children as illustrators

children as illustrators

Making Meaning through Art and Language

Susan Conklin Thompson

photographs by Keith Thompson

National Association for the Education of Young Children
Washington, DC

National Association for the Education of Young Children
1509 16th Street, NW
Washington, DC 20036-1426
202-232-8777 or 800-424-2460
www.naeyc.org

Through its publications program the National Association for the Education of Young Children (NAEYC) provides a forum for discussion of major issues and ideas in the early childhood field, with the hope of provoking thought and promoting professional growth. The views expressed or implied in this book are not necessarily those of the Association.

Carol Copple, *publications director;* Bry Pollack, *senior editor;* Malini Dominey, *design and production;* Catherine Cauman, *copyeditor;* Natalie Klein Cavanagh, *editorial associate;* Leah Pike, *editorial assistant.*

Library of Congress Control Number 2005921345
ISBN 1-928896-22-7
NAEYC Item #2002

About the Author

Susan Conklin Thompson is an associate professor of education at the University of Northern Colorado. She has worked extensively with children as an elementary school teacher, parent, and university professor. Susan has authored numerous articles, seven books for teachers, and two books for children, including *Folk Art Tells a Story: An Activity Guide* (Teacher Ideas Press) and *Natural Materials: Creative Activities for Children.* She has been the recipient of several university awards for teaching excellence and outstanding research and scholarship and in 2001 was awarded the Early Childhood Professional of the Year Award by the Wyoming Early Childhood Association. Susan has also served as an NAEYC consulting editor.

Keith Thompson is a photographer and hydrogeologist. He has illustrated five books with his photographs and has coauthored two books for children. His photographs have won several awards.

This book is dedicated to my children, Kayenta, Rosalie, Yoselin, and Flor de Maria, who love to write and create art. Since they were young they have worked with every illustration technique in this book. I also want to thank young children everywhere, from whom I have learned not only much about illustrating writings but also about the wonderful freedom of expression.

Contents

The young mind generates the impulse to take hold of the world, to understand it, and to bear witness to its wondrous wealth. Once we have acquired the respect for this early achievement, we shall never underestimate the importance of art work at any level of human maturity, be it in the school child or in the adult artist.

—Rudolf Arnheim, *Thoughts on Art Education*

Preface

When I was young, I lived in Cortez, a small town in Southwestern Colorado that borders the Ute and Navajo reservations. My experiences growing up were rich in culture, art, and the outdoors.

Living in the Southwest among the American Indians, the red dirt and canyons, the sagebrush, piñon, and fruit trees, my senses were satisfied and I was complete. From the time I was young, I was fascinated by the designs on the shards of 1,000-year-old Pueblo pottery that the plows uncovered as they tore through the fertile soil of the bean fields in springtime. The reservation trading posts were filled with intriguing and beautiful rugs, pots, jewelry, and folk art. As I grew older, I understood much better what individual artists were communicating through their pieces, and that their artistry represented generations of beliefs and traditions.

I remember clearly the first time I saw pictographs, figures scratched deeply into the surface of the rocks. One figure looked like Kokopelli (a figure playing a flute), and another like a deer and a hunter. I gazed for a long time at the figures, telling and retelling myself a story of what might have happened and what the symbols might mean. Throughout history, humans have represented their experiences symbolically, reading and interpreting symbols in order to connect with others and capture the human experience.

Children create symbols regularly as they strive to capture events and make meaning of their lives, and because it is an interesting thing to do. As a mother, I find drawings by my children in crayon on the sides of boxes, in the sand, and chalked on sidewalks. Such drawings are not only art but also early forms of children's written communication. The drawings tell a story and, as temporary as some of them are, they represent the artist who created them, if even only for a short while.

Some of the most wonderful stories are told through art, and some of the most expressive pieces of artwork are created by children. Much can be communicated through art, and when art is used to illustrate writings in a way that enhances what is written, even more can be expressed. In classrooms today, children are illustrating the stories that they write. When emphasis is placed on illustrating the story along with writing it, children can explore a wide variety of ways to effectively communicate to an audience.

This book, *Children as Illustrators,* explores the process of children illustrating their stories and poems. I first became cognizant of this process when I was a first and second grade teacher. My understandings grew when I had young children of my own and they wanted to write and create books almost every day and then read them to our family. When I became an elementary education professor, I found myself working with teachers in their classrooms and teaching preservice teachers about this process. Understanding children is a journey; the more I learn, the more I appreciate how children acquire literacy and use language in a variety of ways as they express and communicate complicated thoughts and ideas. When we engage children in the world of writing and illustrations, we all receive a gift: a community rich with language, appreciation, and communication.

Writing this book has been a very interesting project, from which I have learned a lot. I thank the people who inspired me with their ideas and who were generous with their time and talents. Thanks to Keith Thompson, Rosalie Thompson, Kayenta Thompson, Yoselin Thompson, Flor de Maria Thompson, William Conklin, Gretchen Young, Kallie Young, Hannah Young, Tom Smucker, the Nganga family, Kathy Swingle, Carol Stewart, Tulip Titus, Sue Berchenbriter, Laurie Paronto, Ginny Harmelink, Joan Bangen, Susan Rea, Barbara Chatton, Zephaniah Joe, Lynn Dart, and the many classroom teachers and student teachers who shared their ideas. I would like to thank Beth Wilkinson and my mother, Mary Conklin, for their love of children and literature. Also thanks to my wonderfully supportive editors, Carol Copple and Natalie Cavanagh, who believed I could write this book and guided me throughout the process, and to the other editors who worked on this book, Bry Pollack, Catherine Cauman, Leah Pike, and Malini Dominey. Special thanks to the children who let me include their writings and illustrations. And thanks to young children everywhere, who amaze us with their writings and illustrations and inspire us with their ideas.

About this book

My hope for this book is that readers will follow children's lead and support them as they communicate their ideas through writing, oral language, and art. Writing, illustrating, and oral language work hand in hand, all being powerful forms of communication. In order to talk effectively about illustrations, I have included information about all three in this book.

Children can express themselves in many ways through visual art, which can involve rebus, collage, painting, and a variety of other media and techniques. They can use visual art to illustrate their ideas and stories. Commonly, when we speak of children as *illustrators*, we envision children using illustrations to enhance or help tell a story, or we think of engaging children first in creating an illustration and then adding text to enrich the illustrations.

This book is primarily written for teachers of kindergarten and the early primary grades. Teachers of preschool children will also find a wealth of useful information and practical suggestions for use with younger children, although some techniques will need to be modified. The material presented in this book is developmentally appropriate for young children and follows the guidelines for developmentally appropriate practice outlined by NAEYC.

Over the years I have tried all the ideas in this book with adults and with children, talked with numerous teachers about young children's writing and illustrations, and taught graduate classes on this topic. I have also observed and talked with children in many different classrooms in 17 elementary schools during the development of this book. The understandings I have gained through all of these experiences are woven throughout the text.

This book is divided into four main chapters, plus a techniques chapter at the end. The first chapter discusses children as creative beings, and includes examining the role that play has in art, developing art experiences for children that are child-centered, and examples of how children create art from their experiences. Chapter two focuses on the connection between art and literacy, discussing how to promote children's learning with book activities, by supporting oral language development, and through observing children as they illustrate and write. Chapter three is about nurturing a love of writing and illustrating and helping children learn from adult illustrators and artists. Chapter four brings the writing and illustration processes together through reflections about and examples of conferences, teachers documenting children's growth, and how children bring oral language, writing, and illustrations together to communicate their ideas and experiences.

Chapter five describes techniques that professional illustrators use, which children themselves can select from to illustrate their own writings.

One of the main strengths of this book is all the examples of children's books provided throughout. All of the children's literature mentioned in the text is listed in the Resources section. As you help children illustrate their writings and examine books by other authors and illustrators, you will have many more favorite books to share with children.

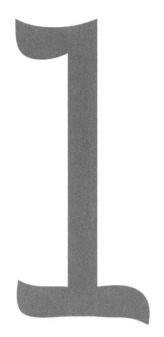

Understanding Children as Creative Beings

A four-year-old child slowly pushes both hands through a wide smear of blue paint on the large painting before her. Swirling her fingers around and around, she is so engrossed that she doesn't notice her teacher sit down quietly beside her. Finally the child pauses. Leaning back from her creation, she notices her teacher smiling at her. "I see you're working very hard," the teacher says, "Can you tell me about your painting?" Looking up with a shy smile, the girl says in a soft but animated voice: "The wind came down and blew ALL around!"

Like this child, young children everywhere love to explore the materials available to them and to express themselves creatively. One's relationship to art begins in these early years. The attitudes developed during childhood about creativity and artistic ability carry over into adolescence and adulthood, dramatically influencing interest in art and confidence in creating it throughout life. Thus it is important for young children to have opportunities to express themselves freely and experience positive feelings and success in art activities.

Children, Art, and Exploration

When children are young, they experiment with different art processes and materials. Schirrmacher (2002) tells us,

> In the early years, children's creative functioning emphasizes a process orientation. The emphasis is on making and doing rather than on

completing a project. For example, children may paint but end up throwing the picture away or not claiming it to take home. The primary satisfaction is in the processing, the smearing with paint, rather than in what it turns out to be. (7)

When we see young children use paintbrushes and water to paint on the side of a house or on a fence, we see them enjoying the process, not the product. Process-oriented activities, such as reading children a book about flamingos and encouraging them to represent flamingo colors with paint, help children connect what they learn to the world around them.

For many teachers, shifting the focus of any project to emphasize the learning process rather than the product is difficult. They experience pressure from families, colleagues, and others in their schools and communities to have children complete identifiable products. Many early childhood educators fall into the trap of encouraging the young children in their classrooms to create something discrete that others can understand and appreciate, such as in the following example:

During a second grade unit on the ocean, the teacher introduces an activity using clay. "You can mold the clay into any of the creatures we studied that live in the ocean or on the ocean floor. When you're finished, you can put your animal in the back of the room to dry. Now watch me. This is how to work with the clay. First I roll the clay into a ball, then I pinch eight long tentacles and make a round head. I pinch the clay to form the beak, and then I use a pencil to poke two eyes. On each of the tentacles. . . . "

After the octopus demonstration, each child receives a hunk of clay. To the teacher's dismay, the children do not seem interested in creating ocean creatures. "They wanted to roll the clay into snakes, pinch it, stretch it, and push objects from the room into it to make impressions," she complains later to a colleague. Then she laughs and says, "I guess I should have given them a chance to play with the clay first. I don't think they ever worked with clay before, and they wanted to experiment with it."

Teachers often feel that a finished product reflects positively on them as teachers and is a tangible representation of children's learning. They are afraid that when children don't bring home projects representing their learning, parents will wonder whether learning is taking place. Educating parents and others about the value of process, documenting what children learn through play and their own artistic experiences, and recording children's conversations are all techniques teachers can use to help others understand the value of the learning that is taking place.

Children need the chance to explore materials.

Focusing on process provides the means for children to express themselves. Self-expression in art is most likely to take place when children are involved in meaningful activities, when the creative process is valued, when there are many opportunities to explore different materials, and when children are allowed and encouraged to discover art elements such as line, shape, and texture (Kieff & Casbergue 2000). During the creative process children play with ideas and materials, learning and practicing new forms of creative expression.

Play and Art

Young children construct knowledge about their everyday environment through play. As children play they gain understanding of themselves, their friends, and the world around them. Play also helps children deal with disturbing events, which they portray through their play. Play provides opportunities for children to learn and work through ideas, being just who they need to be at the time they are playing. As Jones & Reynolds (1992) relate,

> Young children learn the most important things not by being told but by constructing knowledge for themselves in interactions with the physical world and with other children—and the way they do this is by playing. (1)

Isenberg and Jalongo (1997) state that play is the essential style of learning for children. Play experiences with appropriate materials lead to intellectual growth and help children become better problem solvers as they use the information they have gained to confront new challenges (Hughes 1999). Piaget (1951), Vygotsky (1978), and other theorists (e.g., Sutton-Smith [1967]) argue that development of symbols and symbolic capacities, which takes place in children's play, contributes to language, concept formation, and other aspects of intellectual functioning. Play also allows children greater control over their environment and activities as they leave reality to engage in higher-order thought processes.

Play in art can be about exploring materials—a three-year-old sponging paint on sheets of newspaper, experimenting with different colors; a young child adding a drop of food coloring to a bowl of water; children blowing through a straw into a puddle of paint or splattering paint with a toothbrush. In *Children, Play, and Development*, Hughes (1999) describes a child playing with and exploring clay:

> Aaron is busily playing with a large lump of clay. He pounds it repeatedly against the table, then pulls off a large piece, breaks it into several smaller pieces and rolls them into balls. He soon grows tired of rolling,

Play is the essential style of learning for children.

and so he flattens the balls into pancakes, which he distributes to each of the other three children seated at his table. Later he collects his pancakes and stretches them into hot dogs. Then he rolls them into balls again. Next he takes some of the balls, breaks them in half and makes smaller balls of the broken pieces. Finally, when he begins to tire of the clay, he rolls the balls together in the following manner: First, he combines two small ones into a larger one; then he repeatedly adds another ball to the growing mass until he has a fairly large lump, which he proceeds to join to the original lump of clay that the teacher had given him. (178)

Involving children in concrete manipulation of materials keeps them in touch with concepts that many adults know only through vocabulary. For example, young children have informal knowledge about items floating in water through playing in puddles and floating toys in the bathtub. Their knowledge is not expressed through language such as *surface tension* and *density*, although it is important not only to involve children in play but also to give them some vocabulary related to what they are learning. In the example above, Aaron gained firsthand knowledge about the physical properties of clay, learning that while he could change its appearance radically it would always remain the same quantity (Hughes 1999, 178–79).

Examining textures indoors and outdoors can also be part of children's play and exploration. Discovering and collecting natural materials with interesting textures and using them to make prints and collages, or finding small objects in the classroom and pressing them into playdough to make patterns, make for exciting, engaging learning experiences.

Play in art can be about working through feelings and events—a young child playing outside with friends draws chalk pictures of her dead goldfish on the sidewalk to help her process its death; or a child whose family has recently moved paints a picture of his old house. These children are playing with creating and refining their own narratives via an artistic process. Kieff and Casbergue (2000) explain that "Children develop the ability to identify and clarify their own feelings as they express them through art materials and techniques" (174). "Their paintings, drawings, collages, songs, stories, and constructions reveal what they see and understand about the world around them" (173).

When two or more children engage in social play with clay, tissue, paper, fabric, or other art materials, they share ideas, expand their imaginations, and enhance their social skills. What is shared and learned is then added to a child's knowledge bank and encourages additional experimentation. Art activities that are meaningful to children can provide this forum for their constructive and creative play and learning.

Modifications and Adaptations for Children with Special Needs

Teachers need to be intentional about supporting the learning and development of children with identified disabilities or special needs. Following are descriptions and examples of research-based types of modifications and adaptations. Although these modifications were developed for children with special needs, some modification types are helpful for any child who is not making expected learning or developmental progress, as well as for English-language learners. Specific art-related examples have been added for some strategies.

1. Environmental support: The teacher alters the physical or social environment or time schedule/expectations to promote a child's participation, engagement, and learning.

• For example, if a child has difficulty putting materials away during cleanup, use pictures or symbols on shelves and containers. Make cleanup a matching game.

• If a child has difficulty playing near peers, plan cooperative small-group activities with engaging and highly motivating materials so that the child is in proximity to peers while engaging in activities such as murals.

• If a child has no play partners, build friendships by seating the same peer next to the child every day at a planned activity such as small-group or circle time.

2. Materials or equipment adaptations: The teacher modifies materials or provides special equipment so that the child can participate as independently as possible.

• If the child has difficulty standing at an easel, lower the easel and give the child a chair, or cut the legs off an easel and place it on a table. A tabletop easel can also be made out of a cardboard box.

• If a child's feet do not reach the ground in a regular child-sized chair, place a stool under the table that he can rest his feet on and stabilize his body. This stability helps children to more easily use their fine motor skills.

• If a child has difficulty using two hands to act on materials, stabilize materials using tape, Velcro, nonskid backing (such as bath mat appliqués), and clamps. For example, tape one end of the paper to the wall or table for cutting.

• If a skill or response required is too difficult for a child, modify the response. For example if a child has difficulty turning the pages of a book, glue small pieces of sponge or foam to each page; this will separate each page, making it simpler to turn the pages.

• If a child finds gluing and pasting too difficult, use contact paper or other sticky paper as backing for collages. The child only has to put things on the paper.

• If a child has a hard time grasping markers and paintbrushes, add a piece of foam or layers of tape around the markers and paintbrushes to make them easier to hold.

• If a child has visual impairment, use high-contrast materials.

3. Simplifying the activity: The teacher simplifies a complicated task by breaking it into smaller parts or reducing the number of steps.

• If a child is overwhelmed by illustration projects, place only a few materials out on the table at a time and break down the activity or technique into parts. Describe the steps in clear terms: "First we do (x) and then we do (y)," etc. In some cases, you might draw pictures of steps to make the technique even clearer.

• If a child has difficulty understanding stories, use objects or flannel board pieces that represent characters or objects in the story. The child may make connections between the physical objects.

4. Using child preferences: The teacher identifies and integrates the child's preferences for materials, activities, or specific people so that the child takes advantage of available opportunities.

• If a child has difficulty making transitions from one area or activity to the next, allow the child to bring along a favorite toy.

• If a child has difficulty engaging in new activities or learning new techniques and tends to stay with only one activity, incorporate the child's interests into the new experience. For example, if the child loves her dog and has dictated a sentence or two about it, you might encourage her to make an illustration using yarns and fabrics to show how furry the dog is.

5. Adult or peer support: The teacher intervenes or joins the activity to support the child's level of participation; or the teacher uses peers to increase the child's participation.

• If a child repeats the same actions over and over without making any changes, use adult support. For example, if the child always uses only one color in drawing or painting, the teacher can encourage or assist the child to try another.

• If a child is watching two children work in the art center and seems to want to join them, ask the two children to invite the child to join them.

• If a child is learning to use words to request items for an activity, suggest that she ask a peer to pass the item she needs ("Jen has a red crayon she isn't using. Can you ask her for it?").

Adapted from *The Head Start Leaders Guide to Positive Child Outcomes: Strategies to Support Positive Child Outcomes* (Washington, DC: U.S. Department of Health and Human Services, Administration for Children & Families/Head Start Bureau, 2003), 114–18.

Matisse's Special Need and His Paper Cutouts

Children will be interested to learn that a number of famous artists have had disabilities to deal with. When the painter Henri Matisse became ill and was too infirm to paint standing in front of an easel, he changed his working process and medium. Confined to his bed or a wheelchair, he began to make large collages with shapes he cut out of papers that had been painted by his studio assistants.

Many children enjoy using paper in their art explorations and are interested to see a photograph of Matisse sitting in his wheelchair, holding a piece of paper in the air and cutting it with scissors. They see that the desire to make artwork can overcome a disability.

© Elisabeth Nichols

Adapted, by permission, from R. Althouse, M.H. Johnson, & S.T. Mitchell, *The Colors of Learning: Integrating the Visual Arts into the Early Childhood Curriculum* (New York: Teachers College Press; Washington, DC: NAEYC, 2003), 92. Copyright © 2003 Teachers College Press. All rights reserved.

Child-Centered Art Activities

Open-ended activities allow children to express their ideas and build upon their own experiences, bringing these experiences into their art. In an open-ended activity, there is no right or wrong way to work, and there is no one "correct" end result. An art activity of this type reflects the diversity of the group, as children have the freedom to express their individual narratives. Children are engaged because the art has meaning and they can learn about their friends by observing and talking about one another's art.

Activities that are not open-ended have a "correct" outcome predetermined by the teacher. There is no opportunity for the children to express individuality. A "closed" art experience is strictly limited to focusing on a product rather than allowing children to exhibit their uniqueness through their art.

Envision the following two kindergarten classrooms, where children are creating paper jack-o'-lanterns for Halloween. The teacher in the first classroom leads the class through an activity with one, expected outcome; the second teacher engages children in an open-ended project.

Mrs. Roberts passes out orange construction paper with a pumpkin stenciled on each sheet. She tells the children, "I want you to cut out the pumpkin. Be sure to cut carefully along the lines so that the pumpkin keeps his round, cheerful shape." The children cut out the pumpkins; they all look the same.

Then Mrs. Roberts distributes stems, eyes, noses, and mouths she has precut from black construction paper. The children glue the features on their pumpkins. Most glue on the shapes in the typical locations, but two of the children in the class glue on the features in very unorthodox ways. When Mrs. Roberts tapes the pumpkins in a line along the wall to display them she excludes these two children's pumpkins because they are not done "correctly."

This teacher controls the art exercise, leaving little room for individuality or self-expression. She dictates the materials, the process, and the product. Jones and Reynolds (1992) note that "in classrooms where children's work all looks alike, the children are practicing their teacher's ideas" rather than working out their own (83).

By contrast, Mr. Mortimer's more open-ended approach in the following example allows children to be creative and intellectually active. He gives them the opportunity to consider the subject and try out possi-

This child's pumpkin was not done the "correct" way.

bilities before they begin their pictures. Mr. Mortimer provides some background knowledge and then encourages the children to draw from their own experiences. The art activity is integrated with literacy learning, as children scribble or write letters of the alphabet and dictate to communicate their thoughts.

Mr. Mortimer finishes reading Linda Williams's book *The Little Old Lady Who Was Not Afraid of Anything* to his class. He and the children talk about the significance of pumpkins, jack-o'-lanterns, and Halloween. The children talk about their Halloween experiences.

Then Mr. Mortimer puts out paper, crayons, watercolors, and paintbrushes. He asks two of the children to put jars of water on the tables. He suggests that children design their own jack-o'-lanterns—ones they might want to carve for Halloween. They can practice drawing faces on the back of the paper—happy faces, funny faces, scary faces, silly faces. "If you don't want to make a picture of a jack-o'-lantern, maybe you'd like to draw a picture about fall—something like pumpkins growing in a field or Halloween night in your neighborhood or trees with fall-colored leaves."

Later Mr. Mortimer tells the children, "When you finish your picture, you can write about it—maybe your pumpkin's name or a story about it or a Halloween poem. As I walk around the tables, you can read me what you've written, and I'll write it out again at the bottom of your paper."

Experiences in which children are not highly directed by teachers— often called *child-centered activities*—can also focus on children's natural interests. For example, many children are very interested in animals. Using their natural interest as motivation, one teacher challenged the children to find some material in their homes that looked shaggy—like an animal's fur—and then bring it to the classroom. In preparation for their "shaggy" hunt, she talked with them about different textures of coverings on animals. Showing them a large animal book, she had the children point out different animals' coverings such as the wrinkly hide on elephants, the fuzzy fur on a koala bear, and the bumpy hide of an alligator. When she got to the camel, children responded with "hanging down hair" and "shaggy." Then the teacher went on and spoke with children about where they might see different shaggy materials in their environment. Children came up with everything from coconuts in the grocery store to the frayed edges of burlap feed sacks. Their assignment for that night was to find some piece of shaggy material and bring it to school the next day. "If you can't find anything in your home," the teacher said, "you might try looking around outside." The next day the children brought their items in with excited anticipation. After the children shared what they brought and why they thought their material had a shaggy attribute, the teacher asked them what they knew about camels.

Many children knew that camels had large, flat feet, but they were surprised to learn that the wide feet kept the camel from sinking in the sand. The teacher demonstrated this concept by having a child push her finger down into the sand in the sand table. Then she gave the child a flat dish and asked the child to push her finger into the center of the dish and observe what happened with the dish. When the dish did not push into the sand, she had the child offer ideas on why this happened. "Because the plate is bigger and flatter than my finger," was the girl's response. "That's right," said the teacher. She then explained that the camel's wide feet prevent it from sinking in the sand. She went on to dispel the children's misconception that camels carry water in their humps, explaining that camels can go up to several months without water in cool weather but only a week during dry, hot weather. "The hump actually is a large lump of fat (weighing up to one hundred pounds), and if a camel cannot find food, the fat will provide the camel with enough nutrients for it to live for a while."

Camels made from shaggy materials

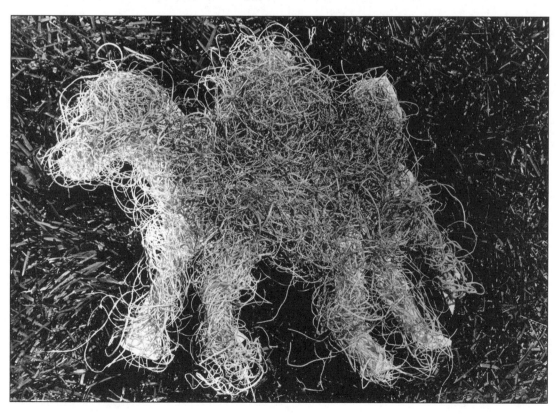

After the camel discussion, the teacher handed each child a piece of stiff paper, and each child cut out the outline of a camel. Then each child glued his or her "shaggy covering" onto his or her camel. The camels were admired by the children and teacher and the class discussed the different materials children used. "That camel looks like the rug in my room," stated one child. "That straw one looks just like a camel I saw in the zoo," added another child.

When children engage in art activities, they bring both their prior knowledge and the shared knowledge they acquire from their learning in class. As explored in the next section, children's experiences and learning build a body of knowledge they can draw on in their creative projects.

Children Create Art from Their Experiences

Learning takes place when children make connections between new experiences and what they already know—knowledge already learned at school or experiences they bring with them from home. If a new school experience is so separate from what they already know that they have no background knowledge to build on, then it does not set children up for success (Dudley-Marling & Searle 1991). In the following vignette, the teacher uses a shared experience (a lost dog) as a jumping-off point for a classroom project and discussion because she knows that the children will come to the project with a common knowledge base. The activity is more meaningful to children and moves them along in their learning, helping them gain new understandings and use language to explore their ideas. It also meets several necessary learning objectives, such as punctuating sentences and using writing to record an event that has taken place.

The children in Mrs. Randle's second grade class are laughing and running around the playground, playing with a large, black dog. When they come in to begin the school day, the dog comes in with them.

"Whose dog is this?" Mrs. Randle asks.

The children explain that the dog was on the playground when they arrived that morning. They all agree that he is a gentle, nice dog.

Acknowledging that the dog seems nice, Mrs. Randle stresses that it can be dangerous to pet or play with stray dogs. "The school has to call the dogcatcher to come and get any dog that is on the playground," she tells the children, explaining that the dogcatcher will try to locate the dog's owner. When the dogcatcher arrives, the children watch through the

A child's dog book

windows as he leads the dog away. They are still excited and animatedly
   discuss their experiences with the big, black dog.

Mrs. Randle takes advantage of the encounter with the black dog to engage the class in an art and writing assignment about the morning's
   adventure. Each child will make a dog book. Mrs. Randle passes out
   white construction paper and shows the group how to fold the paper in
   half. Then she draws an outline of a dog on the folded paper, with the
   dog's back along the fold. "You could make your dog any way you like.
   Some part of the dog, though, must be on the fold so that you will end
   up with a dog shape that opens," explains Mrs. Randle. When each
   child has drawn a dog and cut it out, Mrs. Randle hands out squares of
   white paper for pages in the dog books. The children are to write about
   what they experienced when the dog came to school that morning. Then
   they can use crayons to decorate their dogs.

When the children are finished with the art and writing, they look at each
   other's books. "The dogs are all different, but there was only one dog!"
   states one girl.

Mrs. Randle and the children discuss how it is that everyone could experience the same event in such different ways. She connects this idea to books, telling the children that several people can read the same story and each will see it differently in his or her mind. "When an artist illustrates a book for an author, the illustrator and author have to work together closely, otherwise the author may be very surprised by the illustrations," Mrs. Randle tells the children.

The children read aloud their dog stories and talk about why they created their dogs the way they did.

There are times when teachers need to build experiences for children. If a teacher wants to involve children in an activity that requires some background knowledge, experiences can be designed for the children that will provide them with a common knowledge base from which to draw.

> At times, school experiences may be so far removed from students' experiences that teachers may need to help them build up the necessary background knowledge through the use of presentations, films, books, field trips, discussions, and so on. . . . [T]eachers will be best equipped to help students make the necessary connections if they know them well enough to be able to link the learning with their lives. (Dudley-Marling & Searle 1991, 68)

For example, Wyoming is known for ranching. However, many children I had taught in Wyoming had never been to a ranch, seen cattle being branded, or watched sheep being sheared. One spring day I took a group of children on a field trip to a ranch outside Laramie, where the children met and interviewed Tom Rogers, a sheepherder. The children were fascinated hearing about life as a sheepherder on the Pitchfork Ranch. Tom spoke about his Navajo childhood in Arizona herding sheep and goats with his family and living in a hogan (a traditional one-room Navajo house). The children loved hearing about how he and Shaggy Bear, his dog, herded sheep down the hills, keeping them together. Some children asked Tom whether he felt lonely, and he told them he was used to being alone. The children toured his sheep wagon and compared it with their homes.

Back at school, children painted pictures of their visit with Tom. Each picture was different, reflecting the children's personalities, modes of expression, and different understandings of the visit. One child painted a stylized quilt square with lines representing stitches and white sheep centered against a blue sky. Another showed Tom with his sheep wagon and his sheep, with hills in the background and trees all around. A third showed a boy outside a hogan watching a sheepherder walking by, herding his sheep with a brown and white sheep dog. This rich, rewarding experience gave the children a starting point for their art, and the illustrations reflected each child's learning.

Learning from resources and teacher guidance

Sometimes children want or are asked to work on projects about unfamiliar topics—topics they are learning about that are outside their realm of experience—and need help finding a starting point. Resources to help build children's familiarity with a topic include guidebooks, museum exhibits, and magazines such as *Smithsonian Magazine* or *National Geographic*. These resources offer photographs and realistic models, dioramas, and drawings. Access to such resources enriches children's learning, which in turn changes the nature of children's illustrations. A child illustrating his handmade book about dinosaurs may enjoy creating pictures of dinosaurs from his memory of books, films, and other sources featuring dinosaurs. Or he may wish to create more detailed or realistic

A child's personalized record of her field trip experience.

A Teacher Helps Children Make a Cultural Connection through Art

When children cannot visit people in their environment, teachers can use books, videos, classroom guests, slides, and artifacts to help bring others' experiences to life.

During his practicum teaching, a student in my social studies methods course wanted to involve the kindergartners in his classroom in a meaningful activity about children of another culture. In earlier classes I had talked about Guatemala and discussed folk artists, including Mamie Deschille, a Navajo artist who creates cardboard cutouts of Navajo people authentically dressed in velvet and silk traditional clothing. The student decided on an activity in which the kindergartners would dress cardboard cutouts to look like themselves and then send the dolls to children in Guatemala.

To help young children in Wyoming connect to Guatemalan children, life, and culture, the student borrowed slides and artifacts from my visits to Guatemala. The kindergartners were fascinated. They discussed a classroom in Guatemala with a dirt floor, empty of decoration and books. They commented on the Mayan children's colorful garb. They were awed to see a parrot sitting in a tree in the background of an outdoor slide.

The student teacher prepared the cardboard cutouts in advance. The children searched, sorted, and experimented with tissue paper, wallpaper samples, fabric swatches, and construction paper to dress their dolls. They were deeply involved in the activity. "They're for children in Guatemala," explained one child. "They don't have dolls like we have."

The children completed their dolls with pride, satisfaction, and new knowledge about another culture. Some children had difficulty relinquishing them. On my next trip to Guatemala, I delivered the dolls to a local mission where they where distributed to children in the village.

drawings, in which case he would benefit from access to realistic models of dinosaurs to hold and examine.

Children draw and create what they know. The more learning experiences children are exposed to, the more ideas they will have to write about and include in their illustrations. "Young children rely on memories, images, experiences, and concepts when they draw and paint" (Schirrmacher 2002, 116). Young children's experiences are naturally limited. Children growing up on a farm may have daily chores related to farm animals but no experience with public transportation or personal knowledge of skyscrapers. Some urban children may not know where eggs come from or that clay is an earthen product.

Talking with children about what they see and experience, reading to them, and providing opportunities for them to observe the world in new ways are activities teachers can offer to broaden learning and help children to make new connections. Children can then demonstrate some of these new connections through art, writing, and discussion. Here, for example, is a kindergarten child explaining his composition depicting buildings in his hometown, informed by a class discussion:

> First I drawed a tall building, then I drawed a cop station, then I drawed my house, and then I drawed a movie place. I cut out a picture of people crying and glued it in the movie

because it was a scary movie. I drawed all these things just like we talked about and learned are in my town.

Along with drawing, children can capture their ideas, learning, and experience by keeping writing notebooks where they record their stories and observations. Teachers can be models, writing simple children's books based on their own experiences. In an early childhood course I teach on basic art methods, for example, one student wrote and illustrated a model book about a little lamb whose wool shrank after he fell into the water. When she shared the book with the children in her class, she explained that the story was inspired by an incident at home: A sweater she had knit using lambswool shrank into a very small, toddler-sized sweater when she unintentionally dumped it in the washing machine with her other laundry. After reading her book to the class, she involved the children in making their own books, modeling the processes involved to create a blank book and record one's story in it. In this teacher's classroom, the children were able to record their own writing; teachers of younger children can take dictations. Modeling the process of writing and illustrating an idea in a meaningful way helps children gain mastery over the process themselves.

Learning from people

Field trips and classroom visits from guest experts are critical resources in extending a child's range of experiences to the wider community (Schirrmacher 2002; Capezzuto & DaRos-Voseles 2001; Matthews 2002). Clearly, much of what young children learn is abstract and involves descriptions of experiences they have never known. "When this is the total learning diet, learners become intellectually emaciated, their voices weak. They tend to deny what they know" (Graves 1983, 84). Children's worlds can be expanded and their understandings broadened by meeting new people and interviewing them about their histories, their hobbies, and the work they do. Graves (1983) states, "People possess information. A child can go through 12 years of schooling and never learn to gather information from original sources, people" (79).

Understanding context is a critical part of learning and gives authenticity to writing. The possibilities for learning from others are vast when we listen carefully to what they have to say. Opportunities to interview people and hear their voices make children's writing and illustrations richer in detail and content. I learned firsthand about conducting interviews during my research for *Celebrating the World of Work: Interviews and Activities* (Thompson 2001), and I share my insights with the children I teach.

I discuss with children the challenges of conducting interviews and listening to someone talk about a topic the interviewer has little knowledge of. For example, I asked second-graders in landlocked Wyoming, "How would you be able to write and illustrate a story about a lobster fisherman?" We discussed finding books and magazine articles on the topic, watching movies and nature programs on television, and actually interviewing a lobster fisherman. We talked about using open-ended questions in interviews, such as "What do you like about your job?" and "What would you like to tell children about your work?" I explained the value of using the subject's own words to capture his or her voice. Then, from *Celebrating the World of Work*, I read the story of Gary Parsons, told in his own words:

The possibilities for learning from others are vast when we listen carefully to what they have to say.

> "I am a lobster fisherman and run a business selling lobsters. I started with twelve traps in 1960, and I knew nothing about the business. It was a hobby for me, and I liked it so much that it became my job.
>
> "Being a lobster fisherman is very hard work. I work seven days a week in all kinds of weather. I enjoy doing it and know that the harder I work, the better my business will be. My business has grown so much that today we ship to buyers who sell the lobsters to restaurants and stores in many different states.
>
> "To catch lobsters, I set the traps and leave them for three days. It takes me three days to check all the traps from beginning to end. The traps are baited with pieces of sardines. When I pull the traps out of the water, I have to take the lobsters out quickly. I can handle the lobsters if I don't dilly-dally. If I am slow, I might get bitten.
>
> "One of the most interesting things that happened to me when I was lobster fishing occurred when the movie *Jaws* first came out. It's a movie about sharks that attack people. I was bringing in the main trap and working fast. When I started on the second line, a shark went by. I was really surprised, and it took my breath away because it reminded me of the shark in the movie. He must have been seven feet long and a couple of hundred pounds. Then I saw that he was no longer alive but just looked alive because of the current. The last time I hauled up the trap, he must have been hooked in the rope. I've thought of that shark a lot over the years." (Thompson 2001, 99)

After reading the interview, I asked the children what images came to mind that they could use in writing and illustrating a story about lobster fishing. Here are some typical responses that indicate how deeply the children had become engaged in Gary's story:

"I thought about writing a story about hauling up a trap and seeing a shark."

"I can see the lobsters in the trap all snapping around."

"We don't eat lobsters at my house, but I see them in a tank at the grocery store."

"My mom tried to cook a lobster in the oven on a cookie sheet but it kept trying to crawl off the sheet and out of the oven."

Children also talked about how lobsters are caught and taken to stores and restaurants. Hearing this personal story helped them visualize the lobster fishing process, and they went on to create illustrations with vivid colors and interesting details.

Concrete experiences interviewing individuals make children the experts on the knowledge they acquired from the interview. This allows them to "suspend judgment on something that is concrete, something that is rooted in their own experience. Children take more risks when they have a specialty, a 'learning turf' that has been established in the eyes of other children and the teacher" (Graves 1983, 84).

As teachers, we have the power to foster in children positive attitudes and thinking about artistic ability that will strongly impact their lives and their faith in what they can do. Involving young children in the process of playing with art media as they express their feelings, ideas, and experiences can help the children develop a lifelong interest in, understanding of, and love of art. It is the knowledge and confidence learned through this play process that children carry with them into adulthood.

picking some flowers for my mom

2 Connecting Children's Art with Literacy and Language Development

Illustrations, whether they are done in rebus (using images to represent words), collage, chalks, or other media, should enrich, highlight, and help tell a story. Illustrations can convey thoughts, actions, events, emotions, and experiences to a reader that words may not be able to. Calkins (1994) notes that the approaches to creating art and composing written work are similar:

> In both instances, the composer needs to ask, "How shall I go about making something lovely? What medium might work best?" The artist, like the writer, explores one possibility and then another, drafting and revising. With paint, clay, and fabric, the artist, like the writer, creates imaginary worlds and invites others to live inside them. (87)

In one first grade classroom, the teacher helps children learn a song through the use of images. She says, "When we learn this song today, we are going to replace some of the words with little pictures, and then we will sing it together as a group." The teacher sings the song and then helps the children sing it. On large chart paper she writes the words to the song, leaving blanks where pictures will replace words. She involves the children in thinking of symbols to represent the missing words. "For weather, we can make a snowstorm" and "Draw a bell like a church bell" are some suggestions from children. Interpreting pictorial symbols is an important step on the road to literacy. Experimenting with combinations of symbols and text plays a large part in literacy development, both in reading and in children's illustration and writing.

The Magic of Markers

Children need opportunity for spontaneous expression in writing, and it needs to be free to flow into and out of other expressive activities. Felt pens (markers) are tremendously important. I used to think that crayons would do just as well, but there's something about felt pens—thin ones and thick ones, in many colors—there's a sense in which the children seem to paint with them. There's all that color and brightness and flow, and the colors go on fast and easily. Children can work together more easily around their felt pen drawings, whereas only one child (two at most) would stand at the easel to paint. They talk together about their drawings, and the writing flows out of the talking and drawing. Sometimes the writing gets sloppy, and the children cross out and make blots. But children seem to much prefer felt pens to pencils, and they love to use them in illustrating books. They even decorate the text as well as illustrating it. These drawing tools enhance the flow of reading, writing, and drawing.

Adapted from D. Armington, *The Living Classroom: Writing, Reading, and Beyond* (Washington, DC: NAEYC, 1997), 118–19.

Additional kinds of writing and drawing materials

crayons (both standard and acrylic)
pencils (both thin and thick lead)
colored pencils
charcoal pencils
chalk
pens
pastel sticks
alphabet stamps and ink pads
computer word processing
computer paint programs

Connections between Drawing and Writing

Drawing is the most basic choice for children's illustrations. It is a good place for children to start before moving on to more complex techniques. During the early years, children use drawing to convey meaning in much the same way they will use writing later (Schickedanz 1999). The connections between drawing and writing are intertwined as children create their own written symbols.

Children can illustrate their stories through drawings created with crayons, pencils, or markers. Children may need adult support to achieve the style and details they want in their drawings. However, as Taunton and Colbert (2000) point out, "art instruction that focuses on representation, detail, or accuracy at a stage when children are prerepresentational or beginning to form symbols is inappropriate and disregards the child's natural sequence of development" (69). A common misconception is that art is about creating accurate likenesses in drawing and that good artists must do this. In fact, art is about self-expression and communication rather than precise representation. Young children have not developed the skills needed to accurately represent the appearance of objects. Their art activities center on exploring art materials, relating their artwork to their experiences in the world, and enjoying the process.

You may have heard children say, "I don't know what I'm going to write because I haven't drawn it yet." Some children are more comfortable starting with illustration and then writing. To accommodate young children who organize their thoughts through drawing, many teachers structure journal writing so that children can illustrate what they are thinking and then write about their illustrations.

If allowed to freely write about and illustrate their thoughts and stories, children will capture their ideas, their understanding of others and the world around them, and their feelings and experiences in extremely interesting and authentic ways. In this way, children's communication has depth. And when children use their oral language skills to explain their work and talk about it with others, adults can truly begin to see the world from the children's perspective and have a better understanding of each child's unique experience and understanding. As Armington notes, "It's a combination of noticing what the children do in activities they find genuinely engrossing and noticing how reading and writing fit in with those activities" (1997, 114).

In one first grade classroom, four children and their teacher are playing pet store in a dramatic play area. The walls are covered with pictures the children have drawn of animals. "Ted's Pet Store" is the name of the shop, as is obvious by the bright red letters drawn by the children on the sign that hangs on the wall. Children's books about animals and stuffed plush "pets" sit on tables around the play area. The children act out the roles of customers buying pets, with the teacher as clerk. Together they explore reading, writing, drawing, and play-acting. The oral language here is rich, the sense of community is strong, and the children represent their thinking through symbolic symbols and dramatics.

"By second grade, writing has often surpassed drawing. Although these children may still find it easier to draw than write, many find it easier to embed meaning into a written text than into a drawing. In early first grade, then, the goal is to have writing catch up to drawing; by second grade the goal is often to have writing catch up to talking" (Calkins 1994, 88). Some children begin by drawing and then move to writing, whereas others start with writing and then add their illustrations. Yessica is a first-grader who is successful in both writing and drawing, and moves back and forth between drawing and writing in her journal. This connection in expression—using both writing and drawing to convey events and feelings—seems to come naturally to her.

Drawing contributes greatly to self-expression and writing. It provides a context for children and their writing and a framework for children's thinking as they write stories or relate experiences. Children can use drawing as a way to organize their thinking and the information

Yessica uses both text and illustration in her journal to describe an accident.

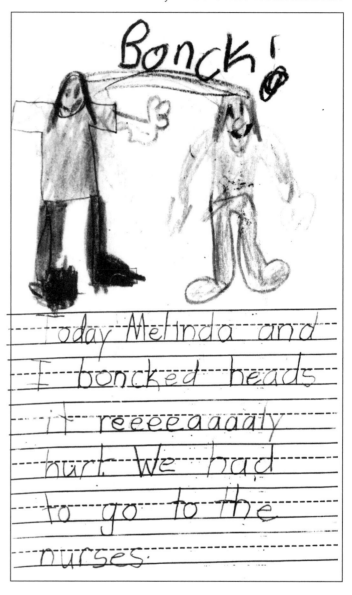

they want to write about. Lucy Calkins (1994, 85) talks in detail about this when describing a young boy, Chris, and how he constructs his writing by drawing his pictures first and using these images to support and scaffold his writing. Chris is relieved to return to his drawing after working with the writing. Back and forth he works, feeling comfortable with the drawings and challenging himself with the writing.

Drawings can also be wonderful springboards for children, affording them a space to work out their ideas and stories through illustration before they write their text. Their writings, discussions, and dramatizations can develop from these drawings, as children add more details and gain confidence in their work.

When children's stories do not lend themselves particularly well to drawings, teachers can introduce or encourage the use of other techniques. For example, it is difficult to create a breathtaking sunset with a pencil or even markers, but a child may make a striking background of reds, yellows, and golds using overlapping tissue paper or watercolors. (Both are described in the Techniques section, beginning on p. 77.)

Observing Children as They Illustrate and Write

Much can be learned from observing children as they write and draw, as the following scene recorded by Dyson (1993) demonstrates. Observations of children working in small groups can be tape recorded, videotaped, or written down. This type of documentation is valuable in that it allows the observer to listen to and/or carefully watch interactions between children, children working on and talking about their writing and drawings, and subtle exchanges in the classroom that take place but may not have been observed at the time they happened. This type of documentation can also be used periodically to assess children's growth. In the following scene, Dyson has carefully recorded interaction in the classroom, allowing for greater insight into the children's symbolic interpretation of their experience.

> Lamar and his kindergarten peers are stretched out on the classroom rug drawing pictures for their alphabet books. Lamar is sprawled between James and Tyler, who is lying next to Anita.
>
> "Louise," Lamar calls to his teacher. "Just like houses. Louise, this is just like houses."
>
> "Just like houses?" asks his perplexed teacher.
>
> "Yeah," says Lamar. "Cause we're all next door neighbors. Tyler is my next door neighbor, and Anita is Tyler's next door neighbor."
>
> "No," objects Anita, "Sonya is my neighbor."
>
> "But in school," explains Lamar. "Not in real life."

"We're not talking about real life," adds James. "We're talking about fake life."

"Yeah, fake life," agrees Lamar. . . .

The children's spaces, explains Lamar, are like houses, and as they work next to each other in the classroom, they become neighbors. Moreover, as Anita makes clear, classroom neighbors are not necessarily "real life" neighbors. But through the construction of symbolic worlds—"fake lives"—relationships between people can be reconceived and transformed into new possibilities. (Dyson 1993, 1)

I documented the following dialogues in a kindergarten classroom while children wrote in their journals. Each day, children sit around small tables and write in their journals. Observing children during their conversations and journal work offers important insights into their current skills and abilities in literacy as well as their social development. As the children in the following dialogues worked together, they moved easily between drawing and writing while they communicated their thoughts and ideas, all the while constructing their own social worlds.

Tim: How do you know what to write about?

Clay: I just sit here and think. I usually write about wildlife because I like it, but today I'm writing about my friends. I could

Focusing on Both Message and Medium

Sometimes children are more comfortable with one means of expression over another. They may be more comfortable with oral language rather than drawing, or prefer drawing and painting to writing. These preferences can change, influenced by ability or mood. While there are a great many learning benefits from the integration of writing with art activities, we must respect that children have their own individual means of expression. Engel (1995, 23) details how six-year-old Jonathan is entirely comfortable conveying his idea of a sunset through painting. He resists the suggestions of his teacher, Mr. Illsley, to further interpret his ideas through writing.

Mr. Illsley: That's a beautiful painting you've done there, Jonathan. If you're finished, perhaps you'd like to write about it now.

Jonathan (*with some annoyance*): Mr. Illsley, if I had wanted to *write* about it, I would have written about it. I wanted to *paint* it!

While Jonathan was conscious of his choice of medium and sure of his reasons for not choosing another, there may be other instances in which the reasons a child selects one medium over another are less clear. Teachers need to recognize when a child needs scaffolding in order to gain skill and confidence in a means of expression the child might otherwise avoid. Cadwell (1997) relates the difficulty in encouraging a child named Michael who was reluctant to engage in any kind of artistic expression. In contrast, this child was a leader during conversation. At the beginning of the year, Michael's mother related that her son "hated" art. As the child's teacher, Cadwell tried several approaches to encourage him to use visual means of recording his observations. She found what succeeded was proximity to a peer who was comfortable with artistic expression.

I decided to see if Michael would sit at a table next to Jessica and try some leaf drawings. . . . Michael told Jessica and me that he couldn't draw a leaf. I said I was certain that he could. Jessica agreed and began to draw with a medium-point black marker. Michael watched her look at the leaf and begin to make lines go in and out to define the lobes of the leaf. He saw that Jessica had invented a way to use the pen that would match the curves of the oak leaf. He decided to try. He looked carefully at the oak leaf he held in his hand. Slowly and tentatively, he followed the curly edges of the leaf with his eye and his pen. He began to draw. When he finished, he was thrilled with his results. (75–76)

In this case what Michael needed was to observe the method employed by a successful peer. Jessica acted as a model and provided the support Michael needed to get started in his own mark-making.

write about something I'm going to do, like go to Kansas City tomorrow, but I don't know what I would write about because I haven't been there yet. So I'll write about my friends. Once Larry, he just wrote a design, and it turned out to be something he wanted to write about and he did.

Not all children are as verbal as Clay, but they do have a lot to say as they draw or write in one another's company (Cocking & Copple 1987). I heard many conversations between children in which they questioned each other about how they decided what to write about. The children were intrigued with what their friends thought about and how it was showing up in their writings and drawings:

(Clay begins drawing two children.)

Sarah *(sitting next to him and pointing at his picture)*: Who is that?

Clay: Logan.

Sarah *(pointing to the face with her pencil)*: He doesn't have a nose.

Clay: I just haven't drawn it yet. *(Adds nose.)*

Sarah: I'm drawing about a mother and daughter and we just came back from Pizza Hut.

Clay: Is the mother and daughter you and your mother?

Sarah: Uh-huh.

Jim: *Up, up,* how do you spell *up*?

Sarah: Sound it out, Jim. I know how to spell that—it's easy. Just spell *up* *(points to the ceiling)*, or just make an arrow up.

Clay *(addressing Logan)*: What color do you want your hair? I'm going to put yellow and brown together.

Sarah: You can draw the hair whatever color you want. I'm going to make my mom's hair green. Once she dyed it blue when she was a teenager. *(Looks at her own drawing and begins talking about it.)* My mom took me to Pizza Hut and I got my clothes all messy. Every time I go to Pizza Hut I get my clothes all messy.

(A boy across from Sarah is working on a story. He leans over to Sarah and asks, "Ming . . . how do you spell this?")

Sarah: Is it *min* or *ming*? *Min*—I'm looking for that letter. *(Meaning N, she looks to an alphabet chart on the wall.)*

Clay: I'm going to write, "It is my friends, and my friends are Logan, Chance, and me *(begins to label drawings, pauses, then goes to the shelf* *and gets the name catalog, which lists the names of all the children in the class for reference).*

Logan: Sarah, how do you know how to spell *pizza*?

Sarah: Everybody knows how to spell *pizza*.

Clay (*starts singing*): How about you, you, you/ Go to the zoo, zoo, zoo. . . .

(Sarah joins in and together they sing two choruses. Singing stops, and Sarah reads her story as she writes.)

Sarah: "I got all messy. My mom is crazy." (*Turns to Clay*) What else should I write?

Clay: You can write "We are happy" or "She is nice."

I got all messe
Mi mom is crase

The process of drawing and the picture itself provide supportive scaffolding for writing. Children ask for help and then use the strategies they have learned to find the spelling of friends' names or to locate the letters they are sounding out. As they look at the word wall, in the name catalog, and on the letter charts, they have the security of knowing that their pictures are still there, providing the framework for their stories. Children switch back and forth between drawing and writing, all the while discussing and thinking together.

The writing period is a social time when children watch one another's growth in the telling of stories. During this "social work," children are interacting with their peers and controlling their relationships (Dyson 1993). The children have a broad understanding of writing. Clay and Sarah are social learners, constructing their social lives together as they interact and share experiences, songs, and ideas from their lives outside of school. Sarah dominates—all the children ask her for spelling help. Yet there is symbiosis, because Clay, who has a good idea of what he wants to express, soon takes a leading role. When Clay sings, he takes control of the situation in a playful way. Sarah joins in, giving Clay the respectful attention and responsive participation he offered her earlier. Clay then has the confidence to assist Sarah in her writing.

Here is another writing session that same week:

Ralph: Look what I wrote about yesterday (*flips back in his journal and reads*).

John: Do you just think in your head and kind of come up with ideas to write about?

Ralph: What are you going to write about?

John: I can't tell you because you'll write about the same thing.

Amanda: I'm writing a picture about one of those games with the ball and you have to try to get it in the middle. Do you know what I'm talking about? There are three balls so that means there has to be three holes.

John: Where are the three balls, though?

Amanda: Right here.

John *(leans over and counts them)*: One, two, three.

Hannah: What can I write about?

Amanda: You can write about playing outside. You can write about anything!

Cheryl: You can write about what you did yesterday.

(John is drawing a horse and Amanda is drawing her game, when suddenly Amanda leans over and points to John's horse.)

Amanda: When they sleep, they do this. *(She gets off the chair and imitates a horse sleeping; then she leans over and points to his picture.)* They bend their knees a lot.

Ralph: What do horses eat?

John: Hay.

"It's a horse unless I decide it's a llama."

Children as Illustrators

It is not uncommon for children to change their stories to fit their drawings, even to accommodate accidents or shortcomings in their work (Cocking & Copple 1987). Here we see how John adapts his narrative to reflect what he has actually drawn and adjusts it for the audience:

Charles: You're writing about a horse?

(John looks at his drawing and is quiet for a moment. The neck on the horse is fairly long.)

John: No, it's a llama. It has a long neck—horses don't have long necks. Maybe it's a dinosaur.

Amanda: Well then, you lied. You said you were making a horse.

John: It's a horse unless I decide it's a llama. *(He writes under the horse, "It is a hors. He is etin ha. It is Suny.")*

(Amanda writes, "It is a gam! It is cool to pla wif a gamm." Then she looks at Ralph's picture of two alligators fighting.)

Amanda *(with respect, commenting to John)*: Ralph is an artist.

John: Hey, what about me?

Amanda: You are, too.

Amanda *(to Ralph)*: What are you writing about?

Ralph: A green and white alligator fighting. I just have to find a few words on the [word] wall.

These children are very interested in what to draw and write about, giving others ideas to develop. Dyson (1993) writes that "the written texts of five- and six-year-olds are often multimedia affairs, interweavings of written words, spoken ones, and pictures" (4).

In this writing session, drama is also incorporated in the interactions when Amanda jumps up and demonstrates how a sleeping horse stands. The children connect strongly with each other through discussion and dramatization. John looks at his drawing and decides it is a llama or maybe a dinosaur, even though he stated earlier that he was writing about a horse. He "lies," according to Amanda, changing the story to fit his drawing. Vivian Paley explains, "The five- or six-year-old is at a singular period. He is not a captive of his illusions and fantasies but can choose them for support or stimulation without self-consciousness. He has become aware of the thinking required by the adult world but is not committed to its burden of rigid consistency" (1981, 80–81). John takes control of his writing and illustrating, stating, "It's a horse unless I decide it's a llama."

This conversation takes place at another table in the same session:

Gayle: I'm drawing my friends, but they aren't at the school.

Jesse: Hey! Aren't you writing about us?

Gayle: No.

Jesse: You said you were! You lied then.

Gayle: Then I will tomorrow. I have to think all night about what to write about.

Diego: Not all night! What if we forgot when we were asleep?

Gayle: Well, we think all night. We just think it up in our heads.

Friends commonly appear in children's writing and illustrations. Children want to be acknowledged by their friends. They strive for social connections and validation of their places in the school neighborhood. Gayle works for harmony with her friends. Diego does not accept Gayle's logic that it will take her all night to think about what to write; Gayle then tries to justify her idea. We can see in their questions and responses that the children are listening very carefully to one another.

Stories and Oral Language Development

Telling stories and listening to the stories of others is important for children's oral language development. As the previous vignettes demonstrate, children's narratives and understandings are constantly influenced by others. Whether conveyed through conversation, storytelling, reading, or book exploration, the language and ideas children are exposed to become a body of knowledge that helps them interpret and understand their experiences in the world. Their new understandings are applied to their illustrations and writing as well as to their interpretations of art and symbols.

"There's a bridge, Mama! I wonder if there is a troll under it," exclaims my three-year-old daughter, Yoselin, as we hike in Rocky Mountain National Park. "Let me look under there and see," she adds as she peers beneath the bridge. "I'll be the troll under here, and Papa, you be a goat. Rosalie can be a middle goat, and Mama can be a goat, and all of you can trip-trap across my bridge." We proceed to act out the story of The Three Billy Goats Gruff, which evolves as my husband becomes another troll under the bridge and Rosalie and I become horses.

In a kindergarten classroom, children are having a similar conversation as one boy assigns parts for his story and then directs the children acting them out as the teacher reads the story he has dictated to her: "He carried a whole bunch of apple seeds everywhere he went. He weared a pan on his head. And at fall he went back home. At the end we singed his birthday." This story-acting approach is best known through the eminent educator and author Vivian Paley, as demonstrated in her book *The Boy Who Would Be a Helicoptor* (1990).

As I observe student teachers in various classrooms, I notice that the time for children to engage in oral language is limited. Yet, the importance of rich language in the classroom cannot be stressed enough. Dudley-Marling and Searle (1991) state,

> In the classroom, the teacher has a key role as language-environment builder. That environment is shaped by the purposes for which students use language and the kinds of audiences available to them. When we successfully introduce authentic purposes and varied audiences into classroom talk, we, in effect, introduce our students to powerful language learners. (37)

In a healthy learning environment, everyone is a teacher and a learner (Calkins 1994) and talk flourishes. A community of learners is rich in language, a place where students can own their learning and work together, where teachers listen carefully to them, where children can respond, read, question, challenge, and share, scaffolding each other's learning (Bredekamp & Copple 1997; Dudley-Marling & Searle 1991). Learning communities are created through talk, and they begin with an atmosphere of trust "in which students feel free to speak and express their ideas without fear of correction or ridicule" (Dudley-Marling & Searle 1991, 64). A community where children feel safe to share and learn from one another is based on support, trust, and cooperation. Children understand that everyone has something to share because the teacher believes that each child has important things to talk, write, and draw about. The more children feel like they are participants in a community, the more they will talk; and the more they use language, the stronger the community will be (Dudley-Marling & Searle 1991).

Young children are beginning to understand that drawing and writing are talk that is written down. As Jalongo states, "They (children) are learning how to think symbolically and how to use pictorial and written symbols to represent their ideas. Particularly for young children, drawing and writing go together because both are ways of expressing ideas and feelings" (2003, 124).

A community of learners is rich in language.

At age three Yoselin is beginning to understand this and uses her knowledge in various situations. Bringing three magic markers and her snow boots to me, she asks, "Will you read my name?" She wants me to write her name in the boots, like we did previously in her coat, so that everyone at school will know they are hers. I think her request to "read" her name in the boots indicates that she knows we read written words and can make symbols that represent her specifically. Her request shows a spark of literacy understanding.

Pictures tell a story

When children are in literacy-rich school and home environments, they learn early that stories can be read, acted out, and written down. They also begin to understand that a story can be told with pictures alone. *The Snowman*, by Raymond Briggs, and numerous books by Mitsumasa Anno (among them, *Anno's Journey, Anno's U.S.A.*, and *Anno's Magic Seeds*) are examples of wordless books to share with children. Another wordless picture book, *Window*, by Jeannie Baker, is illustrated with collages constructed of wood, clay, and other natural materials. (For a classroom activity with a similar theme, see "Natural Materials Collage," p. 108.)

Illustrator Giles Laroche suggests that children think of a story and then make six pictures on six sheets of paper. After they have finished the illustrations they can then link them with text to create a story (G. Laroche, personal communication). This helps children learn to organize their stories according to the sequence of events and reflect on story structure. The story should be able to carry itself without the text, or the child can add words after the story is told through the pictures. Although Laroche suggests this process as an exercise, the pages can be stapled together to create a finished book for children to enjoy.

Reading comic strips with children can also be useful. The comic strip format offers a simple story with the main ideas or events laid out in sequence. Working with this format helps children gain experience with the sequential nature of stories and the use of words and pictures together to convey a story.

Taking culture into account

In some cultures, pictures that tell an entire story are created in striking murals and beautiful religious art, sometimes temporary, which may be used in ceremonies. While children may benefit from exposure to such stories and artwork, teachers must ensure that they are introduced with respect for the related culture and traditions. For example, the traditional healing designs used in many American Indian sandpaintings are sacred and should not be copied. The intricate Navajo sandpaintings created during healing ceremonies tell the stories of generations of healing ceremonies and represent an ancient culture that is still strong today. It is important for children to understand and respect the significance of religious sandpaintings and to appreciate but not reproduce the designs. Teachers can involve children in painting a story with sand in a similar manner, creating designs and pictures that relate to their own experiences. (See "Traditional Navajo Sandpainting: Telling a Story with Sand," p. 117, for suggestions about introducing and conducting a sandpainting activity.)

When discussing illustrations in books with children, help them identify whether or not the illustrations are authentic. For example, in one popular picture book a Navajo hogan is drawn to look more like a log cabin instead of the many-sided dwellings commonly found on the Navajo Reservation. Explain that it is very important that the illustrations truly reflect the culture and traditions they depict.

In classrooms where the children speak or are learning more than one language, it is useful to read aloud bilingual books. If possible, invite family members or people from the community into the classroom to read in other languages spoken by the children. In a classroom where many children spoke Navajo, the class enjoyed having Ann Nolan Clark's book *Little Herder in Autumn* read to them in both English and Navajo. The book features text on each page in both languages. Teachers may be able to find books in other languages that feature English text on one side and an additional language on the other, which are worth looking for. There are, of course, many excellent books that have been translated into Spanish and other languages.

Teachers may want to be wary of maintaining separate collections of books, English versus other languages. This can sometimes be problematic, as separating the books into two or more sets can create a situation where children's choice of books is led by the language rather than the story. In a second grade classroom I visited, one small section of a bookcase held books written in Spanish, while a larger bookcase was filled with books written in English. "Those books are for the kids from Mexico," announced a small boy when he saw me examining a book in Spanish. Pointing to the larger bookcase, he added, "Those are for us."

Featuring text in English and in an additional language near each other (whether on the same page or opposite), such as in the book *Tortillas para Mamá*, allows for the story to lead the children's choice rather than the language. The story is for *all* children and becomes the central focus of the book. This helps prevent the "us and them" attitudes already developing in the small boy above. Children who have two languages may be interested in writing a story in English and in their home language. For example, a child may write his story in Spanish and later write the same story in English, or choose to put both Spanish and English on one page.

There are many rich opportunities in storytelling and art activities for children to explore one another's cultural backgrounds, ideas, and beliefs. As Schirrmacher states,

> Children do not create out of a vacuum. They need a source of inspiration or an experiential background from which to draw. For example, a child who has never visited an airport or been aboard a plane will have difficulty discussing these concepts or incorporating them into block play, dramatic play, movement, art, and other creative activities. (2002, 9)

Art should not be an isolated classroom activity. Instead art activities should be planned in a way that allows and encourages children to express who they are and to gain a greater understanding of the world.

Using Books to Help Children Connect Art and Writing

Young children are experiential learners. Teachers can facilitate greater comprehension of the books children read by engaging them in in-depth explorations of a book's topic. There are many ways to investigate a topic, both before and after a book is read. Children can explore related materials and props as well as generate their own written and illustrated responses, all of which enhance the total learning process. As Harste and Short (1991) relate,

> When readers move from reading to writing or from reading to art or drama, they take a new perspective on the piece of literature. In the process of trying to express their interpretation of the literature through various sign systems, they discover new meanings and expand their understanding of what they had earlier read. Students need the chance to respond to literature in a variety of ways over time. Their responses become more complex and reflective when response is not seen as a one-shot affair. (196)

A third grade class in Wyoming is preparing to read Peter and Connie Roop's *Keep the Lights Burning, Abbie,* a book set in Maine. Most of the children have no idea what life is like in Maine. Many have never been to the ocean, a major theme in the book. The teacher wants to help children gain a better understanding of the ocean before they begin the book.

The teacher announces that Doug has something to share with his classmates. From his desk Doug takes a small wooden chest about a foot long. He opens the lid of the chest. Taped inside the lid are postcards with pictures of the ocean. The chest holds shells of different colors and a plastic bag filled with sand. Doug tells the class, "My father lives in Washington State, and he wrote me a letter that he sent with this chest. He said that every day he walks along the beach and thinks of me. Each day he picks up a shell to send to me. That's why there are all these shells in the box." Doug walks slowly around the classroom and lets each child peer into the chest.

The teacher explains that Abbie might pick up similar shells in Maine, although she lives by the Atlantic Ocean, not the Pacific. The children find Washington on the wall map of the United States, and then they find Maine. The teacher passes around some shells and stones she has collected at the beach for children to examine. She explains that the stones have been worn smooth by the abrasive action of the water rolling them against the sand. The children take turns feeling sand in a pail. "People say you can hear the ocean in this large shell," the teacher explains, holding a conch shell to her ear. Sounds of waves crashing and seagulls crying can be heard on a nature tape playing in the background. The children talk about the sounds they hear.

With the teacher's help the children set up an ocean still life. They place a basket of shells on the table. While the ocean sounds play, the children use acrylic crayons to draw ocean scenes from their imaginations. Later, the pictures will hang in the hall. Remarkably, the seascapes capture the mist of the ocean, seagulls flying high overhead, crashing

Postcards can serve as additional sources of information.

Postcards Enhance Creativity

When onsite visits and firsthand experiences related to book topics are not possible, postcards and artifacts can increase children's comprehension, build cultural literacy, and serve as inspiration. Make a habit of collecting postcards when you travel or visit museums, and ask your friends and the children in your classroom to do so as well. You can build a wide and comprehensive postcard library with which to supplement children's reading.

For example, for children reading Jeanette Winter's *My Name Is Georgia*, about the American artist Georgia O'Keeffe, make available postcards with photographs of lush flowers and souvenir postcards from the Southwest—steers, sheep, the desert landscape, adobe houses, and ancient Indian glyphs on the side of a cliff. These images expose children to some of O'Keeffe's influences and the sources of inspiration for the giant flowers and dried, bleached animal skulls she painted. Add postcards featuring reproductions of her artwork, especially the pieces not shown in the book. After children read about O'Keeffe and absorb the flavor of the postcards, encourage them to paint colorful oversized flowers or create landscapes inspired by photographs of New Mexico.

waves, and the expansiveness of the open water. This teacher's approach was clearly effective in helping children gain a better understanding of the ocean.

Whenever possible, teachers can display authentic artifacts with books. Artifacts help capture children's interest, build understandings, and bring a book to life. For example, a small Navajo rug placed beside the book *The Goat in the Rug, as Told to Charles L. Blood and Martin Link by Geraldine* gives children a chance to hold and examine an authentic Navajo weaving. They can observe the dyes and feel its weight and thickness, then learn about the weaving process in this engaging tale.

Similarly, placing a small Peruvian wall hanging, or *arpillera*, with Arthur Dorros's book *Tonight Is Carnaval* enhances children's appreciation of the book. (A teacher might find an *arpillera* in a store selling Peruvian or South American crafts.) This story of a Peruvian family going to a carnival, and what takes place when they arrive, is illustrated using photographs of *arpilleras* from Peru. Children can examine this piece by a Peruvian artisan, observe the connections between the *arpillera* and the illustrations in the book, and reflect on the cultural authenticity in their writing and illustrating. Having them create fabric collages of their own would be a natural way to extend children's learning after reading the book. (See "Fabric Collage," p. 109, for ideas about a similar art activity.)

Promoting children's learning during read-aloud sessions

Children will benefit from discussing how stories and illustrations work together, but first they need to be exposed to the possibilities for observing and analyzing illustrations. Reading books aloud to children and modeling the process of looking at the illustrations and text is a good beginning. Here are several examples of how teachers can guide children's learning during read-aloud sessions. In the first one, the teacher is introducing the book *Joseph Had a Little Overcoat*, for which illustrator Simms Taback won the Caldecott Medal:

"Simms Taback took an old Yiddish folk song called 'I Had a Little Overcoat' and added beautiful illustrations," Mr. Miller tells the class.

"As I read the book aloud, I want you to pay special attention to the illustrations and see if you think they go well with the song. Also see if you can figure out how the illustrator created the illustrations."

Related objects such as the textiles in these displays add value.

A teacher reading another Caldecott Medal book frames the discussion like this:

"Lon Po Po is a Red Riding-Hood story from China, written and illustrated by Ed Young. Before we read the story, I want to go through the book with you and look at the pages to see what the illustrator, Ed Young, has done with the illustrations. As we look, see if you can find a wolf on all the pages. Also notice how the illustrations are very important to the story—the text is just off to the side, on top of the background. See what else you can notice about the illustrations."

In this first grade classroom, the teacher discusses Pat Hutchins's *The Doorbell Rang:*

"What do you see again and again throughout the book?" the teacher asks the children.
"There's black and white tiles on the floor and the floor runs through the book," is the reply from one child.
"That's right, the tile on the floor appears on pages throughout the book and pulls the book together for the reader."

Promoting children's learning with book-related activities

Teachers can extend children's involvement with a book through a number of activities to help them reflect on the book and its themes as well as express their ideas and reactions creatively. Brainstorming book responses, children will come up with possibilities such as painting posters to promote the book, molding clay sculptures of the book's characters, performing a play using the characters in a related story, and creating mobiles, murals, original songs, dioramas, poems, and so forth. Teachers can guide children in what responses may work well with different books and help them think about the materials they will need and how they can acquire them.

Children can select a book-related activity from the class's brainstorming list or think of an original one of their own. When the children complete their book responses, teachers can display them in the classroom. Families will enjoy them during a Book Response Night, giving the children an opportunity to share their projects with a wider audience.

Some teachers may feel that formal responses rely too heavily on external reinforcement and structure. Instead they may wish to engage children more informally in responding to books and stories; for example, through conversation and exploring props together at circle time. This may be true especially for teachers of kindergarten and preschool children rather than older children.

Younger children can work on book activities that connect with any idea in the book, while teachers can challenge primary children to relate their projects to the major themes and main ideas of a story. For example, after reading the story of the Gingerbread Man, older children can be encouraged to respond to the Gingerbread Man's personality or confrontations with the animals and people chasing him, rather than involving them in making gingerbread, as we might with younger children.

Here are some book response activities carried out by kindergarten and primary-age children:

- After reading about and studying Hopi traditions, first and second grade children listened to Hopi flute music. The second-graders created paintings of horses, fires for cooking, and Hopi dancers.

- First-graders created their favorite book characters by cutting figures and items out of butcher paper. After drawing and coloring their characters and items with markers, they glued them onto a large piece of butcher paper to create a mural.

- Kindergartners drew story responses following a reading of *The Giving Tree*, by Shel Silverstein. The children used markers to draw scenes from the book and dictated a descriptive sentence that was written down by the teacher.
- A child who had read numerous books about dinosaurs sculpted a dinosaur from clay.

Young children can also be involved in less formal book responses that are very open-ended. For example, following the reading of a book about polar bears and penguins, children can play at the water table with floating plastic foam "icebergs" and plastic polar bears and penguins.

An extended response project

Projects based on a particular book can be extensive and involve the entire class. One unique book response re-created a cyclorama. Cycloramas were a popular form of entertainment in the United States and Europe in the late 1800s, although few remain today. They are murals in the round—huge 360-degree paintings of continuous scenes encircling a

Kindergartners' responses to The Giving Tree.

room, with viewers standing on a platform in the middle. Cycloramas can include actual objects—for example, soil, bushes, and artifacts placed in the foreground would seem to blend into the paintings. Shining a light on a particular scene, a narrator describes the events depicted, and the scenes converge in a dramatic retelling of the subject—a historic event, a religious scene, or perhaps a literary work. An excellent explanation of an existing cyclorama to share with children is Dean S. Thomas's book *The Gettysburg Cyclorama: Portrayal of the High Tide of the Confederacy*. The painting portrays the events leading up to Pickett's charge during the Battle of Gettysburg, a turning point in the Civil War. (For more information check the National Park Service Web site www.nps.gov/gett/gettcyclo.htm.)

A wonderful simulation of a cyclorama was produced by first-graders in response to Chris Van Allsburg's book *The Polar Express*, which tells about a small boy and his wonderful train adventure to the North Pole, where he meets Santa. The teacher divided the children into small groups. Each group prepared a mural for one wall in the room using cut

One side of a cyclorama

Children as Illustrators

paper collage and poster paints on large pieces of butcher paper. One group illustrated the city at night, another painted forest animals in the woods, and the third painted a mountain scene with little elves. The completed murals were hung on the walls around the classroom.

On the morning of the cyclorama's unveiling, the first-graders in the class came to school in slippers, nightclothes, and robes—like the children in the book. To begin their presentation, they lay "asleep" on the floor while dream snow dust (small pieces of white paper) was sprinkled on them.

The classroom lights were dimmed, and the children "woke up" and got in line. Handing the train conductor (the teacher wearing a conductor's hat) their train tickets, they sat on chairs facing the front of the classroom, arranged as if on a train.

The teacher began reading *The Polar Express*. When she reached the passages illustrated in the murals, she shined a flashlight on the appropriate portions of the paintings. Partway through the story, teachers and teacher aides wearing chef's caps served the children hot chocolate, rolling portable trays through the aisles of the "train."

Projects such as this can be important exercises to extend children's learning. They can also help children personalize stories and become creative illustrators themselves. Book activities help children with comprehension and support their creative spirits. Challenging children to invent book responses builds confidence and encourages them to see broad possibilities for linking creative ideas to stories and poems.

✳   ✳   ✳

"Are the young children in my classroom building strong relationships and expressing themselves through play, oral language, writing, and art?" Teachers who answer yes to this question more than likely have rooms where open-ended literacy experiences and play allow children to make authentic connections to the world around them, where children are encouraged in all forms of communication and understand that each form supports the others, and where children are part of a classroom community. Classrooms that celebrate and support children's symbolic expression and communication engage children and help them develop confidence in their literacy development.

Learning from Adult Illustrators and Artists

A kindergarten teacher sits on a small chair, holding up Eric Carle's book *The Very Hungry Caterpillar*. The children are seated on the floor in front of him. The teacher, Mr. Gonzalez, asks the children if anyone has read the book before. No child raises a hand.

Mr. Gonzalez tells the children, "This book is illustrated by Eric Carle. He's the author and the illustrator. Does anyone know what we mean when we say someone is an illustrator?"

One child ventures that an illustrator is a scientist; another says an illustrator is someone who writes words. A child says that the illustrator is a caterpillar, and then another child shouts out that the illustrator is the person who makes the pictures. Mr. Gonzalez responds with "Exactly!" The teacher explains that the person who writes the book is the author, but Eric Carle is the author *and* the illustrator. "Different illustrators use different ways to make illustrations, like drawing or painting." Then he shows children a few of the illustrations in the book and asks them what materials they think Eric Carle used to make the pictures. One child suggests chalk and another suggests paint.

"Any other ways to illustrate besides chalk and paint?" asks the teacher. A child mentions markers and pens.

The teacher nods and tells the children that as he reads the story, they should look at the illustrations carefully to see if they can spot where paints, tissue paper, and other materials have been used.

The children listen intently as Mr. Gonzalez reads, and together they discuss each illustration and the materials used. The teacher explains how overlapping pieces of tissue paper create a collage and that a collage can be made of paper, fabric, or a variety of other materials glued together on a piece of fabric, paper, or board.

Illustrators today create glorious illustrations that capture the essence of what the authors are writing about. When children are exposed to artwork by different illustrators, they discover a wonderful variety of techniques. They can appreciate that when they blow paint or piece together a picture with fabrics, they are learning new art forms. When children use these techniques, they are illustrating their books in some of the same ways that professional illustrators do.

Children benefit from exposure to works by master artists.

Children also benefit from exposure to works of fine art, old and contemporary, by master artists. Children appreciate opportunities to learn more about all kinds of people, including artists. Learning about the history and accomplishments of others, children can appreciate the many types of contributions individuals make, discover role models they can emulate, and develop a beginning interest in cultural history. "When children have the opportunity to talk to, work with, and observe artists and illustrators, they learn that they have much in common with these grown-ups who make a living 'playing around with art.' These experiences help children value and maintain the artist within themselves" (Kieff & Casbergue 2000, 173).

The knowledge children acquire studying illustrators and artists helps them connect to art they encounter in books, museums, public art and monuments, and many aspects of everyday life. A child who has just learned about Gilbert Stuart, "Father of American Portraiture," will notice for the first time the print of Stuart's 1796 painting of George Washington on a wall at school or recognize the portrait on the dollar bill. Learning about artists and their work can be a rich experience. Showing children reproductions of celebrated paintings and discussing them builds knowledge and informs children of techniques they can use in their own illustrations.

Talking to Children about Art

I often wonder about the value for children as young as kindergarten age in learning about artists and art (primarily focusing on learning artists' techniques, but incorporating biographical information as well). In various presentations, Lilian Katz (1990) has commented that young children can do lots of things that we want them to do, but the question is—are they things that young children should be doing? I discussed this with a friend who is a kindergarten teacher, and we decided that she would try introducing the painter Vincent van Gogh and his work to the children in her classroom. We would observe the children's reactions, and my friend would follow up, documenting any children's conversations relating to the Van Gogh discussion that she heard later.

On the appointed morning I went to the kindergarten classroom. The teacher sat in a rocking chair with the children seated on the floor in front of her. On a small easel rested a print of Van Gogh's painting "The Starry Night." The teacher held a photograph of Van Gogh.

Teacher (*pointing to photograph*): This artist was a great painter. His name was Vincent van Gogh. He lived about 100 years ago.

Chloe: I wonder how old he is.

Teacher: Van Gogh was born in a country called Holland. (*The teacher and children look at a globe.*) This is where we are in the United States, and this is Holland. Holland is clear across the Atlantic Ocean.

Salvador: Like where the Leprechauns live!

Teacher: That's right, across the Atlantic Ocean, like Ireland. Van Gogh only lived 37 years. That's not very long, is it?

Chloe: Well, it kind of is.

Teacher: It seems kind of long to you but not to me, because I'm 38.

Children: Wow!

Teacher: Van Gogh loved to paint. He painted 800 paintings.

Jesse: That's almost a thousand paintings!

Avery: I counted to 518 once.

Teacher: Then you know that 800 paintings is a lot.

The teacher related information about Van Gogh to children's prior knowledge. She integrated geography into the discussion. Although finding Holland on the globe is perhaps too abstract a concept for kindergartners, one child related his knowledge of where Ireland was located to the location of Holland. The teacher put the brief lifespan of 37 years into perspective by comparing it with her own age. The children considered Van Gogh's 800 paintings in the context of their experiences with numbers and counting.

Teacher (*indicating "The Starry Night"*): This is a picture of one of Van Gogh's paintings. When we look at this painting, the first thing I want you to observe is what time of the day it is.

Jaden: Dark.

Teacher: It is dark. What's another word for dark time?

Jaden: Nighttime.

Teacher: It looks like nighttime. What tells you in the painting that it's nighttime? Can you find some clues?

Sam: Blue color. It's kind of a dark color.

Teacher: What other colors did Van Gogh use to make it look kind of dark?

Diego: Yellow next to the dark color.

Teacher: You are right! Painting yellow next to blue really makes the dark color show up. Now let's look at the way Van Gogh painted. (*Indicating paint strokes*) If you took a paintbrush and started to paint this picture, how would you describe your paint strokes?

Faith: Little blue strokes.

Teacher: Little blue strokes, yes. What else can you say about the paint strokes?

Diego: Straight and circled.

Teacher: Yes! Some strokes are straight and some go in circles. Are they short or long strokes?

Kayni: Short.

Teacher: You are very observant. That's right, Van Gogh used a lot of short strokes. Do you think he used thick paint or thin paint?

Kayni: Thick, because of the light blue where it kind of looks like people.

Teacher: Yes, thick paint. Can all of you see those strokes in the paint? Now, let's observe another thing about the colors Van Gogh chose. Let's look at the blue, for instance. Is blue a warm color or a cool color? Think of things in nature that are blue. Are they usually warm or cool?

Brandon: Cool! Because of the ocean.

Teacher: That's right. Most of the time we think of water as being cool. Did he use some colors that you would think of as warm colors?

Kayni: The moon.

Teacher: The moon is yellow. Do you have any ideas about what Van Gogh might have called this painting?

Children's paintings, done after learning about Vincent van Gogh

Children: "Spooky" . . . "The Burning House Picture" . . . "Hilltops" . . . "Twinkle Lights."

Teacher: "Twinkle Lights." What's up there in the sky that would make him call it "Twinkle Lights"? You are right on target, because this picture is called "The Starry Night."

Although this is a long, detailed discussion for young children, the children stay engaged and on track as the teacher expertly guides them to new ideas, connecting new knowledge to prior knowledge and building on their experiences. The children's answers are often approximations, which other children react to and build on. Following this discussion, the teacher provides a demonstration involving the children.

Teacher (*holding up a paper plate with finger paint on it*): We talked about Van Gogh using thick paint. Is this paint thick?

Trianna: Yes, because you can hold it and it doesn't run.

Teacher: Could we do this with watercolors? What would happen to the paints then?

Trianna: They would drip down.

Teacher: That's right. This is special, thick paint. It is finger paint, but today we are going to paint with paintbrushes instead of our fingers. (*Holds up two paintbrushes, one with thick bristles and one with thin.*) Do you think Van Gogh used a brush like this or a brush like this to paint thick, heavy strokes?

Trianna (*pointing to the thin-bristle paintbrush*): The red one.

Teacher: He could have used both brushes, but when he wanted to get really thick strokes, he probably used this other brush, the thick one.

Skye: Do we have to paint that Van Gogh picture?

Teacher: Not unless you want to. You can paint a picture like it, with stars or planets if you want. It's up to you. I'm more interested in seeing you paint with thick paint and short strokes, like Van Gogh did. (*She tapes a large sheet of paper to the wall.*) We're going to try this out. Sarah, do you want to demonstrate? (*Sarah walks up and takes the thick paintbrush.*) Show us the way you think Van Gogh painted his strokes. (*Sarah paints a couple of short strokes.*) Yes, they are short strokes! He made some strokes here just using little, tiny, short strokes. (*Pointing to a group of paint strokes in "The Starry Night"*) What do you think these strokes represent?

Children: Wind. . . . Clouds.

Teacher: I hear some good ideas. And down in here? What did he paint in here?

Skye: A house.

Teacher: Yes, little houses made with little, short strokes. Now let's try painting some pictures the way Van Gogh painted, with thick paint and short strokes.

The children learned about other artists throughout the school year, and they remembered some techniques from each. For example, some time later, when the teacher squeezed thick paint onto paper plates for the children to take to their desks, one boy exclaimed, "Thick paint, just like Van Gogh used!"

Learning from Illustrators

I conducted an illustrator's workshop with children in second grade. The children talked about the illustrations by Giles Laroche in Rachel Field's book *General Store*. After studying an illustration depicting many, many items on store shelves, one boy asked, "If the guy who illustrated this book cut out all the things from paper, how did he get them so flat?" This was an opening for us to talk about the illustrator's process in creating the illustrations and the production process in publishing a book. We talked about how Laroche cuts out what he has drawn, paints the cutouts, waits until they are dry, and then glues on more pieces of cut-out paper. He calls this process "paper relief."

When one girl asked, "How does someone else know what to make about somebody else's story?" we explored the idea of one person writing the story and another illustrating it. This led to a conversation about the advantages and disadvantages of authors illustrating their own work. "One friend of mine," I told the children, "wrote a book for children about a boy she knew when she was a child. The book was

Boating on the lily pond . . . Play-acting extends what children have learned about painter Claude Monet and his watercolor technique.

The illustrations in General Store *are made from paper cutouts.*

about his adventures around the neighborhood and funny things that happened to the boy and the author's friends. It was illustrated by someone she didn't know, and she didn't see the illustrations before the book was published. When the completed book arrived at her home, wow, was she surprised! None of the children or even the dog looked like she had pictured them." The children and I then talked about whether they would like to have someone else illustrate their work, and they decided with their teacher to try out illustrating each other's writings at a later point.

Children as Illustrators

Access to Books

In order to benefit from exposure to quality children's literature and illustrations, children need access to such books. Research indicating that middle-class children had better personal libraries at home than many low-income children had at school (Krashen 1997) only reinforced what many educators and activists promoting literacy had known all along—that book ownership matters. Reflecting a growing recognition of the need to give children opportunities to read and own books, interventions are increasing—both internationally, as evidenced by the literacy projects supported by the International Reading Association, and nationally, in projects such as Reading Is Fundamental (www.RIF.org) and In2Books (www.in2books.org). Below are some tips for increasing children's access to books.

Book format. Paperbacks often are one-third to one-fourth the price of a hardbound book, particularly if they are ordered through teacher book clubs such as Scholastic or Trumpet. Thus, you may want to rely primarily on inexpensive paperbacks when building a lending library. That way, if a paperback book is accidentally ruined, the loss will not be as substantial. You may want to keep certain books, such as those with moving parts or copies signed by the author, on a teacher's shelf, reserved for supervised use with young children.

Book use. Teaching and demonstrating the proper care of books, rather than expecting children to know automatically how to handle books, is important. For young preschoolers, show them how to turn a page, then offer some guided practice with a book that will not cause too much upset if a page gets wrinkled. Demonstrate how to operate the pull tabs or pop-ups in a book without ripping them. Give children a chance, with gentle coaching and supervision, to operate books with moving parts. Be aware, also, that even older children may not have much book-handling experience.

Book lending. A good idea is to invest in some heavy plastic bags with zipper-type closures and have families use them for carrying books back and forth between the early childhood program and children's homes. This practice can be an effective way to keep the books clean, dry, and out of mud puddles. If you are creating *book packs*—small collections of books and accompanying activities that are centered on a particular theme—inexpensive waterproof containers such as tote bags, backpacks, or small plastic bins make good containers for carrying these collections to homes and around the classroom or center.

Book care and repair. A book whose cover is rather worn can sometimes get some additional use if a plastic book cover is placed over it. Book covers usually are easy to find in stores right before school begins in the fall. If a book page tears, use high-quality invisible tape to fix it. If stray pencil or crayon marks appear, try using an art gum eraser to remove them. If the cover is falling off, duct tape placed carefully along the edge where it won't obscure the pictures might keep it together long enough to circulate a bit longer. When books get sticky or need to be sanitized, try this method: Begin with a clean, dry cloth or sponge. Spray it with disinfectant mixed at the ratios specified on the bottle. Gently wipe the book's surfaces and allow to air dry thoroughly before closing the pages.

Book loss. If a book is never returned despite efforts to get it back, take the attitude that losing a few books is unavoidable, and hope that the book is being loved and used.

Adapted from M.R. Jalongo, *Young Children and Picture Books,* 2d ed. (Washington, DC: NAEYC, 2004), 31, 63.

I had interviewed Giles Laroche about his illustrations, and he gave thoughtful answers to my many questions. I transcribed our discussion and shared his answers with the second-graders during the workshop:

Question: Can you tell me some things about yourself as a child?

Giles Laroche: I was born in 1956 and grew up in Berlin, New Hampshire, in the middle of the White Mountains, which are the first things I remember drawing as a child. Mountains, rivers, trees, and houses were among my favorite drawing subjects, and they still are. I used picture making as a way to understand things and make discoveries. I tried to illustrate as many school projects as I possibly could. As a child, I also enjoyed poring over maps, and reading and gazing at books about faraway lands. Those are the types of books I enjoy creating for children.

Question: Your collages are spectacular. Why did you select a collage technique for your illustrations?

GL: I call the medium I use to create my illustrations "paper relief," because it is a combination of many materials, such as water-based paints, pastels, inks, and a variety of paper surfaces separated by spacers. Each element in my illustrations is first drawn on paper such as Bristol board, printmaking paper, or watercolor paper. Then with an X-acto knife I cut out what I've drawn, paint it, and let it dry before the next element is ready to be glued to it. Eventually, after many hours, I have a finished bridge (or other object) and I'm ready to create its environment and background.

Question: How do you decide which parts of a story to highlight through your illustrations?

GL: In *General Store,* the words in the poem suggested my ideas for the illustrations. For example "kegs of sugar brown and white." However, there are opportunities in books such as *General Store* or *Sing a Song of People* to elaborate. To add people and a refrigerator, shelves, a wooden floor, to show the kegs of sugar in context. Some illustrations can be completed in a week, but others involve me for six weeks.

Calkins (1994) writes about children becoming enamored of an author or illustrator to the degree that they make murals and bookmarks and book jackets celebrating that person's books. I fell in love with the artwork of Giles Laroche the first time I read *General Store,* and I'm thrilled every time I share his work. However, I try to temper my enthusiasm: Children need to discover for themselves illustrators with whom they personally connect. Then they will look for more books illustrated by "their" illustrator, try out some of that illustrator's techniques, and keep

Children enjoy using the same techniques they see in their favorite illustrations.

that illustration style in mind as a benchmark against which they can compare and contrast artwork in other books.

Calkins (1994) also talks about some ways we can nurture reading-writing connections and use children's love for particular authors to inspire them in their work:

- Give children opportunities and experiences through which they can get to know a book or an author very well so that there is a good chance of that book or author influencing their writing.

- Pay attention to the reading-writing connections children are already making and build on them. Story schema and language from other stories children have heard or read will often occur within their own stories, such as in the following opening line of a second grade writer: "Once upon a time Barbie went off to see the world." This provides us with a window into some of this child's literacy experiences and insights into the child's thinking.

- Help children realize that literary effects are the result of an author's deliberate craftsmanship. Listening to a writer's choice of language helps children write in ways that have meaning and reach an audience. For example, in the book *Dinosaurumpus!*, author Tony Mitton draws readers in and helps them imagine the scenes by repeating the phrase "shake, shake, shudder . . . near the sludgy old swamp. The dinosaurs are coming. Get ready to romp." Listening to these words and other descriptive phrases such as "with her snip-snap grin" and "he . . . blunders along with a Bomp! Bomp! Tread," the reader gets a feeling for the sights and sounds of where the dinosaurs are going and what they are doing.

Experience with quality literature and illustration informs children's own work.

These same strategies for connecting to authors can work for children who connect to a particular illustration style and/or illustrator, as well. Multiple exposures to many illustrators and the work that they do can influence what techniques children use when they illustrate their writings. Children who have studied the illustrations of Giles Laroche, Eric Carle, Barbara Cooney, and the like, will have several examples of styles from which to draw ideas for their own illustrations. Experience with quality literature and illustration informs children's own work, helping them to think of different ways to bring life to their stories and impart to them the literary impact they desire. Illustrator Guy Parker-Rees used his illustrations to complement Mitton's writing style in *Dinosaurumpus!*. Parker-Rees's illustrations match the tone of the writing in that they are very descriptive and zany, helping the reader understand exactly what a "dinosaurumpus" looks like. A child reading this book and examining the illustrations and text may be inspired to create a similarly lighthearted and descriptive story.

The skills and knowledge acquired through the examination of multiple artists and illustrators provide children with many ideas for their writing and illustrations. That learning also has the effect of broadening children's understanding both of what an artist is and of themselves as being artists. How gratifying for the children to discover new tools to tell their stories; and how gratifying for their teachers to hear "I can do that, too!"

and Big Max found him.
It's a realy good
book.

Extending Learning through Reflection and Revision

Lupita is inspired by the small, colorful illustrations that form borders around many of the pages in Jan Brett's book *The Hat*. She comments to James, "When I make my book, I'm going to make little pictures around the edges that tell more about the story. Then kids can look at those pictures and know more about my cat. See, if I make a little picture of her bed and her food dish and put them out there like that, then you will know what she eats from and where she sleeps."

Guadalupe decides to make a book with only pictures: "I want to make a book that my little brother can read, and he can't read words, only pictures. Maybe when he is older I could go back and add words; or I could make a new book that is a reading word book to go with this one."

Salvador likes the illustrations in Harriet Zeifet's book *Lunchtime for a Purple Snake*: "These illustrations look like ones I do. The colors are nice, and I can make a snake like that one."

Kayenta exclaims that she's going to make a book about her family: "I'm going to cut out my family and have them above the book and then write about them in the pages underneath."

These four children have many ideas, and they express them freely to one another. They are thriving in a warm, trusting first grade environment. In a comfortable community of learners like this one, children tend to take more risks in all their efforts and forms of communication, whether they are speaking, writing, or drawing. They are more open to learning from one another, nurturing one another through challenges and hardships, sharing one another's joys, and feeling a sense of belonging as they discover themselves within a large group.

As teachers, we can create warm environments where children feel valued. Environments that allow each child to share his or her ideas and life experiences let children know that what they do matters.

Creating a Safe Environment

Ms. Stewart has her first-graders come one at a time to a table and read their stories to her. In these conferences she talks with them about their writing and helps them think about changes they might make. One day she noticed that some of the children held their breath while waiting for her suggestions. After she had talked with several children about their writing, she overheard them tell each other, "I didn't get anything wrong today." Hearing this comment, Ms. Stewart realized that she needed to make the environment safer for the children so they would not feel bad when she told them they needed to continue working on their writing or their illustrations. A safe community gives children the support and comfort they need to grow in all areas of their development.

After that day, Ms. Stewart worked hard when conferencing with children to validate what they had written. She focused her comments on how a change could strengthen their stories, rather than on what they needed to do to "fix" their writing. For example, instead of commenting that a story was hard to follow because the child did not explain how the pig got out of the yard, Ms. Stewart's conversation with that writer went like this:

Ms. Stewart: I really like your story. How did the pig get out of the yard?

Child: The gate's latch wasn't very strong and when he hit the gate, it just opened.

Ms. Stewart: How interesting! It's hard for me to tell that from your story. Tomorrow, when you work on your story, do you think you might be able to tell something about how the pig escaped? It's such an exciting part in the story, I think the reader would really like to learn more about it.

An interactive process in which the teacher and child confer together about the child's work can be risky for teachers, as they risk hurting a child's feelings about his or her work and children may feel vulnerable because of the nature of the conference. However, "the more the teacher and child work together, the more risks can be taken. The challenge to stretch thinking, accept new risks with information, to rethink original intentions can be brought into the conference" (Graves 1983, 114).

Listening attentively to children helps convey respect.

Feedback and Revision

Positive comments are very important to children when they are creating, editing, and revising their writing. Even adults become discouraged when they work hard on a project and then have to make changes. Teachers should, however, try to avoid nonspecific praise—general comments such as "Good job!" are less helpful and tend to direct children's attention to pleasing the teacher rather than improving the work.

Mrs. Young, who teaches seven-year-olds, has found a positive and engaging way to demonstrate the concept of revision. When Mrs. Young begins talking with children about the writing process, she hands out lumps of clay. She asks children to use their fingers to pinch a figure out of the clay. When the children finish their small figures, she asks them to think about how their sculptures changed as they worked with the clay. Mrs. Young then encourages them to make any further changes to their figures that they would like. "You can take some clay away from one part of your sculpture to make it look more realistic or add some clay to another part of your sculpture. Ask your neighbors for advice on what else you can do to improve what you have made," Mrs. Young tells them.

The children turn to one another to consult. Some children who are working on animals change the ears slightly or pinch their elephant's trunk into a different shape. After completing this process, the children proudly share their figures with their classmates.

Mrs. Young explains that improving their writing also involves a lot of work—that by changing, adding, and taking away words they can create a better and better piece of writing. Mrs. Young's method of teaching children about editing and revising by using clay makes the process more concrete for children. It helps them see that their work gets stronger when they stop and think about it and seek others' input. It is hard for children to go back and make changes in their writing, because they consider a piece to be completed after they write it the first time. They tend to feel unsuccessful, like they did something "wrong," if they are asked to make a correction or if a change is suggested.

Mrs. Young also explains that illustrators do a lot of work on their illustrations, too. They work on an illustration for some time until they get it to be just how they would like it, often taking things out or redoing parts of their image. That is, the same attention to detail that we put into our writing can also be put into our illustrations. As with writing, revision does not come easily to children working on illustrations. The value of revision in artwork—reworking illustrations, getting feedback from others, reflecting on techniques—also needs to be demonstrated. Children particularly need support and input as they think about how well their illustrations go with their writing. I tell the children I teach that even illustrators of children's books go through many revisions before they get it right. Professional illustrators find it helpful to have people guide, question, and direct them in their work. I sometimes use as an example a book talk I attended a few years ago.

The book talk was presented by Deborah Kogan Ray, illustrator of *My Prairie Year, Based on the Diary of Elenore Plaisted*, by Brett Harvey. Ray brought with her some drawings she had done for the book. They depicted some of Elenore's family members after spending a harsh year living on the prairie, as Ray imagined them looking. Being from Wyoming, I think I have a fair sense of what it would feel like to live on the prairie in bad weather, being whipped around each day by the wind, and the isolation that would begin to show in a person's face and demeanor. The illustrations conveyed this perfectly.

I was interested to hear that the first time Ray sent her drawings to the editor, the editor returned them and told her that the illustrations did not look stark enough. So Ray reworked them. The second time she sent them in, the editor told her they looked better but still not stark enough. Finally, after a number of revisions, the drawings were accepted for publication.

While my daughter Rosalie was pursuing a degree in art, she illustrated with watercolors a children's book that my husband and I wrote about Lenten processions in Guatemala. The book is called *La bella alfombra de Gabriela (Gabriela's Beautiful Carpet)*. To show children how illustrators revise their work, I bring into class color copies of Rosalie's first illustrations to compare with the final work that appears in the book. The colors in the first paintings were not bright enough, according to the book's editor, so Rosalie repainted them to make them more vivid and give the pictures more depth. I also tell the children how my husband and I, as the authors of the book, reworked our thoughts and our writing as well, visiting many families in Guatemala to collect information. We rewrote the story a number of times until we got it just right.

Research demonstrates that kindergarten children benefit from expressing the same idea repeatedly through drawing (Hilliker, 1998). Repetition in drawing—exploring the same or related topics or themes—allows children to develop and

Creative Art Expression: The Reggio Emilia Approach

There is a growing interest today in integrating art in the early childhood classroom, partially as a result of the widespread interest in the Reggio Emilia approach to early childhood education. In the preschools of Reggio Emilia, a town in northern Italy, the children spend time each day expressing their ideas through art media. Activities stem from the interests and ideas of the children. They have an active part in the planning of the curriculum, and their personal input is shown in their creative art experiences. The result is that children express themselves artistically in a much more mature way than do most children their age (Katz 1990).

In the Reggio Emilia approach, the arts are integrated into the school program as problem-solving activities, rather than as discrete subjects or disciplines taught for their own sake (Wright 1997). Children's art making is emphasized to reinforce concepts, and their art products are considered to represent aspects of their learning. Visual arts are seen as an additional "language," one in which the children's ideas and concepts are expressed in art media (Edwards, Gandini, & Forman 1998).

Perhaps the most innovative activity to evolve from the Reggio Emilia approach is a unique form of documentation. American early childhood educators are familiar with documentation in the form of note taking, videotaping, language experience, written comments, and checklists. However, in the Reggio Emilia approach, documentation in the child's own words is accompanied by artworks or photographs. The documentation panels display the child's work with great care and attention to both the content and aesthetic aspects of the display (Katz & Chard 1996). The documentation describes in the child's own words—and sometimes the teachers' as well—the images, ideas, and processes represented by the child's artwork. The documentation may appear on trifolds, bulletin boards, or charts. The words of the children or teachers are in large print, so that children, teachers, parents, and visitors can easily read them. This form of documentation makes visible the child's learning, since it often shows the processes of the art experience from beginning to end (Cadwell 1997; Helm, Beneke, & Steinheimer 1998; Hendrick 1997).

express richer thoughts and feelings on the theme. As Hilliker states, "[w]ith each redrawing, the meaning that the picture represents for the child becomes more dense and elaborate." Encouraging children to revisit an illustration they are making is also a hallmark of the Reggio Emilia approach (Forman and Fyfe 1998), as described in the box elsewhere in this chapter. Teachers can provide children with a variety of art materials and the opportunity to create several versions of the same idea. Children need to talk with other children and with adults about the development of their illustrations and how the illustrations will be perceived by an audience.

Along with creative opportunities for illustration, children need plenty of time to develop their ideas. They may work on a project for a while, move on to another activity, reflect on the project, and then come back to it—and still need more time to work through the illustration process. As is the case with professional illustrators, adequate time is important for children in achieving the results they strive for.

Putting Writing and Illustrations Together

In many classrooms teachers have children collect their stories in a folder. The children then select the story they want to revise and take through the publishing process to share with an audience. The same strategy can be used for illustrations. After a child chooses a story, she or he can make a number of illustrations and then select which ones to publish with the story.

It usually works best for children to create their illustrations on pages separate from the text. Then if they want to make a change in either the writing or an illustration, they will not have to re-create both. The writing pages and the illustration pages can be bound together or otherwise combined after both have reached a satisfactory point in the revision process.

When children are thinking about how to lay out the story—that is, how to position the text block in relation to the illustration on a page or on two facing pages—teachers can have several books available showing different approaches to layout and design. Two interesting examples are *This Old Man*, by Carol Jones, with circle cutouts used as story clues on the pages, and *Mary Wore Her Red Dress and Henry Wore His Green Sneakers*, by Merle Peek, with its unusual treatment of text within boxes superimposed on the full-page illustrations. Many children's books are laid out with text on one page and the accompanying illustration on the facing page. Another standard page layout places the text block under the illustration on a single page. Children can examine the placement of illustrations on each page in relation to the text blocks in the sample books. Teachers can point out how illustrations do not jump around in a book but appear in a logical sequence and are coordinated with text content, telling a story along with the words.

Determining the sequence of illustrations seems easy to an adult, but children have much more limited experience with books than adults do. To help children understand the sequencing of illustrations and how words and pictures work together to convey the sense of a story and the details, you might involve them in the following activity.

Guide children in folding and cutting a sheet of paper into a lift-the-flap book format (see box). Ask children to draw a picture on each of the four flaps, so that the four pictures in sequence tell a story. Now ask children to open the first flap and on the uncut paper under it, write the words of the story that go with the picture on that flap. Have them do the same for the remaining three pictures. When they finish, they can share their stories with one another or with the entire class.

When children share their stories, have the audience first look at the four pictures and guess what happens in the story. Then the author-illustrator can lift the flaps and read the text. Children will be interested and surprised to find how their perceptions of the story based on only the pictures change after hearing the words. Point out that not only do the words enhance the pictures, but the pictures give the story more depth. Ask

Lift-the-Flap Preparation

This activity may be a little difficult for younger children to follow, so you might want to model it first. Younger children may need the paper folded for them before they cut it with safety scissors.

Fold a piece of paper in half, lengthwise. Fold it in half again, this time crosswise; then fold it in half crosswise once more. Open up the two crosswise folds. Now the paper is only folded lengthwise. The length of the folded paper is divided into four equal parts by the three crosswise creases.

Through only the top thickness of paper, cut along the three creases to the fold. When you are done, there should be four little flaps that can be lifted up, exposing the uncut paper beneath.

The example shown below uses the lift-the-flap format, but its author-illustrator didn't follow the "story" model. Instead, the guess-then-reveal aspect is used to pose a series of riddles: "What lives in grass?" . . . *lift the flap* . . . "Snake."

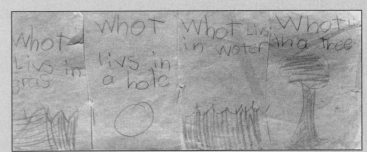

A closed lift-the-flap book.

The inside of the lift-the-flap book.

children what the pictures tell them that the words do not, and vice versa.

When children are creating book illustrations, ask them to tell you about their work. If you try to guess what an illustration is—asking if the picture is an airplane or suggesting that it looks like an airplane, for example—you may influence the child's answer. By listening to a child talk about his or her work, you will learn a lot that you did not know or could not have read into the picture. One three-year-old child drew a picture that was difficult to identify—it looked to me like four distinct lines. When I asked him about it, he explained, "This is me, Papa, Mama, and my brother Bernard." As he explained the drawing and reflected on what it was telling the reader, he added clarifying details to the picture. For instance, when the child got to Bernard, he made little lines going out from the top of the line that represented his brother. "This is his hair," he explained, referring to Bernard's dreadlocks. When I understood what he was expressing through his symbols, I thought about how part of the process of learning to write or draw is not only forming marks, dots, and other symbols but also the child's coming to understand how he or she has placed lines together in order to tell a story.

The writing and illustrating process

The teacher in the following examples is guiding first-graders through the writing and illustration process, reflecting with the children on their work, and allowing them to talk with and guide each other. The process takes place over a three-day period. Working over several days gives children some distance from their own writing and drawings so they are better able to think about them as another reader might.

On day one, the children sit at small tables, several children together. The teacher gives everyone a sheet of paper with three big circles. She invites them to draw and write about three things they can imagine seeing in their neighborhood when they look out a window at home. She instructs the children to draw pictures in the circles with markers and write about the pictures below. These will then be their "story maps," or writing plans.

At one end of a table, Erin draws three stick figures with hair going different ways—her friend and her two brothers. She tells the child next to her about the drawing:

Erin: I see my brothers playing with my friend. I don't know what to write because I can't spell *friend*. I'll write "I see my brothers" and that is good for now. (*Erin writes the shortened sentence and erases the friend.*) I erased the friend because I didn't want to say "and my friend."

Mrs. Joe *(hearing Erin's explanation):* You can write the entire thing and I'll help you with spelling. *(The teacher helps Erin sound out all the words. Erin finishes the sentence.)* Now you can draw that friend again if you want.

Another child at the table, Shelby, is drawing a picture of a duck in the water, with the words *a duck* at the top of the page. The teacher encourages the children to add details to their pictures. Han leans across the table and points to Shelby's picture:

Han: You can make some birds flying around.

Shelby: OK. *(She draws lots of flying birds.)* Now I should write "and birds."

The children move back and forth between writing and drawing as they think through their ideas. Their work evolves as they discuss it with their classmates. At the end of the session, the teacher tells them that the next day they will move on to editing and will think together about what they are writing.

On day two, the children are at their tables and the teacher stands at the front of the room, by the whiteboard. To begin the lesson, she asks the children to get out their story maps and look at what they have written and drawn. Mrs. Joe begins teaching the whole group by addressing Nancy and discussing her writing as an example:

Mrs. Joe: Let's read your story, Nancy. It's about your neighborhood and what you see when you look out your window.

(Nancy reads what she has written below the three circles.)

Mrs. Joe: Let's write the beginning of your story on the board: "My neighborhood has . . ." *(The teacher transcribes Nancy's story on the whiteboard as Nancy has dictated it, then asks the class to read it as she points to the words.)* Now, what is the first thing you are likely to see in your neighborhood?

Nancy: Cars.

Mrs. Joe: Yes, you wrote about cars first. "My neighborhood has cars." What does your next sentence say?

Nancy: It says "I see my dog." *(The teacher writes it on the board and looks back at Nancy.)* My last sentence is "I see a praying mantis."

Mrs. Joe *(writing "I see a praying mantis" on the board):* That's such an interesting sentence. Can you tell the group what a praying mantis is?

> Children move back and forth between writing and drawing as they think through their ideas.

Nancy: It's a bug that has wings, and it goes like this from side to side on a leaf, like praying. (*Demonstrates how a praying mantis sways back and forth.*)

Mrs. Joe: If you want your sentences to sound a little different from one another, you could start this sentence with something other than "I see," because you have "I see" for the sentence about the dog. (*Addresses the class*) What else could Nancy say?

Max: You could say "There are dogs in my neighborhood."

Mrs. Joe: That is a very good idea. I'll write "There are dogs in my neighborhood." Does anyone have a sentence that does not start with "I see" or "I have"?

Emily: I put my third sentence to say "I can see trees in my neighborhood."

Mrs. Joe: I like that. I'll write "I can see a praying mantis." (*Writes the revision using Emily's wording on the board*) Nancy, would you like to make a change to "I see a praying mantis" so it begins in a different way than the other sentences?

Nancy: "I can see a praying mantis in my neighborhood."

Mrs. Joe: I like the way that sounds. So let's see, now you have down "My neighborhood has cars. I see my dog. I can see a praying mantis in my neighborhood." Very nice, Nancy. Now I would like for all of you to see what you have written and see if you can make all three of your sentences begin differently.

The teacher has the children turn their attention to their writing plans, reading and revising what they have written so that their three sentences are different from one another. The children talk among themselves, validating each other's choice of words through listening and commenting:

Kaelyn: I'm going to put "I have a house."

Greg: I can put "I have a house" too, because that's one of my pictures.

The teacher tells them that the next day they will write the first drafts of their stories and work on illustrations.

On the third day, the children sit at tables with their earlier work in front of them. The teacher reviews the writing and illustration process of the previous two days. She tells the children that today they will write a draft of their stories on lined paper and work on the illustrations, using crayons and markers. When they are satisfied with their drafts, they will create their final versions. She instructs the children, "As you work on your stories and illustrations, please confer with each other. Read your draft to the person next to you, and have that person read his or her draft to you. Then give each other ideas. When you are happy with your sentences, you can combine them into your story. You can add other sentences and ideas into your writing if you want to. I'm also going to give you a plain white piece of paper, on which you can combine your pictures to create an illustration to go with your writing. I'll come around and read what you have written and look at your illustrations. When you are ready, I'll give you a piece of paper with lines on the bottom for the writing. In the top space on the paper, create your final illustration."

Here are some of the children's exchanges while working on their drafts and drawings:

Erin (*reading to Alex*): Here's what I wrote: "I can see my brothers and my friend."

Alex: How do we know which of those people are the brothers? Maybe you could color two with black hair and then we could tell they are brothers.

*   *   *

Lance (*has no idea what Tyler's sentence says*): Move this here, Tyler. I forget what it says, but you need to move it.

Tyler: OK, let me erase it and move it.

Lance: Now I'll show you how to spell *houses*. You write H-O-R-I-S.

Tyler: OK, I can write that. I was close. (*Erases "hossis" and writes "horis." Looks up the word in his word book.*) You're right, Lance, only there is no *R* in it.

*   *   *

Nancy (*addresses Gabby*): You copied off mine and made a praying mantis! Maybe you copied off mine because you want to be my friend.

Gabby: I do want to be your friend! (*Both girls are very pleased.*)

*   *   *

Shawna (*to José*): See my drawing? I drew myself on a box looking out the window but on the wrong side. Maybe when I go home I can look out the window on the other side and draw those things. Only then I might see things I didn't already write about.

José: You could still use your sentences about seeing your dog and the grass.

*   *   *

Reyna: Amir, you can move the bees to be in the picture with the truck.

Amir: And I can put the pictures in the circles together to make one picture, with the truck on the grass and the bees flying around in the sky!

At the end of the editing session, the teacher asks the children how their classmates helped them think about things in new ways. Here are some children's comments:

Ashley: We helped each other write more words.

Tyler: I helped Lance with words by telling him where they are in our book.

Jason: Aimee helped me think about another sentence.

Shawna: José helped me add details, like hair on the dogs.

After the children finish working together on their drafts, they write and illustrate their final pages. Their teacher, Mrs. Joe, then combines all the pages into a class book. Mrs. Joe talks with the children about their work and tells them that although they have used markers and crayons this time, there are many other techniques they could try when they illustrate their writing. The children then consider other techniques they could use to illustrate their writing, such as collage, watercolors, or crayon resist.

Talking with their classmates can provide children with valuable feedback. Notice that this teacher asked the children to think together about their writing and illustrations, rather than to suggest changes. When a teacher frames instructions in a positive manner like this, children will work together to revise again and again. One way to support young children's growth in writing, then, is to encourage them to read their writing to other children. They will realize they have more to tell and will add more, including details (Calkins 1994).

A teacher's interactions with children can encourage their thoughtfulness and extend their awareness of possibilities. For example, a teacher might ask a child about different ways to make quilt collages by saying something like this: "Tanya, I like your idea of making collage illustrations that look like quilts. How are you thinking you'll make the quilt pictures?" If the child seems not to have ideas for how to proceed, the teacher can suggest resources; for example, "You may get some ideas by looking at books illustrated with quilt pictures. This is one of my favorites—it's called *In the Hollow of Your Hand: Slave Lullabies,* and Michael Cummings illustrated it with quilt squares. Do you have another idea for your quilt pictures?"

Questions can help children clarify what they want to tell their audience and guide them in thinking differently and exploring new ideas. Sixth-grader Jerome is doing all of these things when talking with seven-year-old Sammy about a story Sammy is illustrating:

Jerome: What is your favorite illustration?

Sammy: I like the Sheridan Hotel, that's why I put it on the cover. And the llama, it's good too.

Jerome: Are there any illustrations you're having trouble with?

Sammy: The drawing of my cousin is kind of messy. I didn't know how to draw her sitting on the ground. Maybe I could just put her on a chair so she would be easier to draw.

Jerome: That's a good idea. Are there any illustrations where you think you need to add more?

Sammy: I like the llama picture. I could put a person riding it, because my cousin rode one.

Jerome: Are your illustrations where you want them in your story?

Sammy: Yes.

Jerome: Do you need borders around your pages?

Sammy: No, I have lots of color because of the stamps all over. Borders would be too much going on.

Jerome: Why did you use markers and crayons for your pictures?

Sammy: They look cool. The cover looks like marbling. I just got my markers from my mom, and I wanted to try them. I like them a lot and could add lots of color with them. (*Now Sammy asks Jerome some questions himself, to get more input on his illustrations.*)

Sammy: Which drawing do you like?

Jerome: I like the goat picture because it has good details, like the grass. I like how you did the grass and leaves and the goat's hair.

Sammy: Do you think any of them need more work?

Jerome: Maybe more snow in the illustration where the car got stuck. Or maybe more than one goat in this other picture, or you feeding another goat.

Useful Teacher Prompts to Engage Children and Extend Their Learning

"Tell me about the ideas you have for your illustrations."

* * *

"Those are such interesting ideas for illustrations. Can you tell me the art techniques you are thinking of using?"

* * *

"What materials do you think would work well in that picture?"

* * *

"That art technique (crayon resist, collage, etc.) is a wonderful idea for that illustration! Will you use that same technique on all the pages, or will you try different techniques on other pages?"

* * *

"What art techniques and materials would best match the mood (theme, etc.) for your story? How could you create illustrations that would create a feeling of happiness (fear, etc.) for the reader?"

* * *

"Would you like to look in some children's books to see how other artists have made their illustrations?"

"And the page showing Chelsie looks happy too."

Sammy: I could draw me feeding it with a bottle. Does my book seem happy?

Jerome: Yes. The page where you got stuck in the snow reminds me of snow and Scooby Doo. And the page showing Chelsie looks happy too.

Documenting Children's Growth

To document a child's growing ability in and understanding of illustration, photocopy or photograph a piece of the child's art a few times a month, date the copy, and put it in the child's file. Return the original artwork to the child to keep in his or her folder. A child's growth in writing can be documented at the same time, as well. When children look through the artwork collected in their folders, even younger children can notice that their drawings and writing have changed. By the primary grades children can do more analysis of how they have developed in their ability to communicate through illustrations and text.

Teacher Ginny Harmelink described to me how she uses photographs of children's artwork to document their growth and the activities they are involved in:

> I keep copies of children's illustrations to show how much the children have grown from one month to another. We do many types of art activities—for example, we recently decorated hats. After completing their hats the children documented the activity by drawing the process. Together we photographed the drawings and the hats with a digital camera.
>
> We distribute these records of our activities to families in the form of a colorful newsletter. Not only is this an engaging way for children to tell a story about what they have done through drawing, but it is also a way to illustrate a newsletter so that it is personal and charming.

I conducted a conference with a kindergarten teacher and a child and was very interested in the insights the child had about her writing and illustrations. The vocabulary she used to describe her work was impressive. She discussed concepts typically used by older children:

Question: Let's look together at the three pieces of writing with drawings you have in here. I see that this one is from the beginning of the year, this one is from the middle of the year, and this one is recent [toward the end of the year]. How do you think your drawings changed from this first one to the next and then to the one you did last week?

Child: They got better. When I drew this one, I was just five and the lady and her dog are floating around in the air. They are also kind of strange colors.

Documentation of a children's art activity

Question: What about this next drawing? What do you think about it?

Child: The people are standing on the ground and the colors seem like they match better.

Question: OK. How about the last one?

Child: This one shows my dad and me flying a kite. His hair is brown in the picture, just like on his head, and we are on the sidewalk. The kite is in the air, but that's where it goes.

Question: So you think your drawings improved over the year?

Asking Questions and Encouraging Art Talk

Teachers can limit children's responses by asking *convergent* questions—questions with one right answer. There is a place for convergent questions when one right answer is required. *Divergent* questions encourage thinking in many different directions and reveal how children think about a problem. For example, the convergent question, "What color did you use to paint this shape?" has only one answer. A divergent question such as "What ideas did you have when you painted these shapes?" encourages children to reflect on the processes they used to develop the artwork. Too often teachers ask convergent questions without realizing that they have limited the children's thinking processes. During art experiences teachers should use the types of questions that will elicit thinking and discussion among children and teachers. In order to challenge children, teachers can ask many open-ended questions about art processes. (See the box "Useful Teacher Prompts" elsewhere in this chapter for some examples.)

Children's answers to questions determine whether teachers need to rephrase their questions or statements. For example, a first grade teacher said to Maria, "I see a dog in your picture." Maria answered in a frustrated tone, "That's not a dog; that's my mama." Realizing his mistake, Mr. Allen responded, "Tell me more about your mother." This gave the child the opportunity to give more details about the picture.

To further encourage children to talk about their artwork, teachers may say, "Please tell me more about your picture" or "What would you like to say about your artwork?" Both examples are open-ended and elicit further discussion. Children's use of language should be accepted. For example, second-grader Isabel said, "I have two kitten in my picture." Ms. Haines responded in a positive way, "Yes, I see two kittens in your picture." Instead of focusing on Isabel's grammar, the teacher had focused on the artwork. Some children speak with a distinct dialect, and teachers need to be knowledgeable about cultural differences in children's language.

How a teacher uses art talk with children and how she encourages them to share art talk influence how well the children express themselves with art media. Some ways teachers can facilitate art expression follow.

Encourage children to reflect on their art experiences. Keep art portfolios and ask questions about their work. "Which picture do you like best?" "Which one did you work on the hardest?" When a child spends several days on a painting, talk to the child about the changes you observe each day.

Use correct art terms. The teacher may say, "You made a secondary color." "How did you make that tint?" "I see you drew straight lines, zigzag lines, and diagonal lines." "Can you point out some free-form shapes in your collage?"

Focus children's attention on the way they use art media. "I see you are drawing circles with the blue marker." "How did you make the sides so high on your clay cup?" "How did you turn your clay into a ball?"

Label the child's actions. "You are pouring blue paint into red paint. What color did you make?" "You are making a shade by adding some black paint."

Introduce new art concepts with actions. Model an art process as you present a concept. The teacher talks out loud: "Oh dear, I want a lighter tint of blue for my sky. Here, I'll add more white to my paint."

Make sure that children understand art concepts and techniques. "How did you make green paint?" "What happened to this line? Where does it end?" "How did you use the lines to make this picture interesting?"

Help children make connections between and among concepts. Use a Venn diagram to compare works of art. The teacher says to the children, "Look at the painting by Claude Monet and the collage next to it by Henri Matisse. What colors are alike? Do the artists use any of the same shapes? What shapes are alike?"

Verbalize a problem and help children find a solution. A child becomes frustrated using a white crayon on white paper, and the teacher asks, "I wonder if we could see your drawing better if we use a different color crayon? What other colors could you use to help you see the lines?"

Connect art with other areas of learning. Children visit a pet store and, as a follow-up activity, use the puppet stage to create their own pet store. They bring stuffed animals from home to sell in their store. They draw and color pictures of animals to decorate their pet store.

Encourage children to talk together about their art and share art experiences. Listen to what children say to each other about their artwork. Encourage children to describe the processes they used to create a product.

Talk with children about artists from various cultures and countries. A teacher might show children artworks of several well-known artists, including Claude Monet, Romare Bearden, and Georgia O'Keeffe. In this manner the teacher introduces children to a French impressionist artist, an African American artist, and a female American artist.

Refer to children as artists. Emily constructed several books throughout the year, and she always signed her name at the bottom of each page like a real artist. The teacher commented, "We show how proud we are of our artwork when we sign our pictures like artists do."

Adapted with permission from R. Althouse, M.H. Johnson, & S.T. Mitchell, *The Colors of Learning: Integrating the Visual Arts into the Early Childhood Curriculum* (New York: Teachers College Press; Washington, DC: NAEYC, 2003), 54–55,136–37. All rights reserved.

Child: My dad's hair got more real and the people and things quit floating in the air, except the kite. But that's where kites go if there's some wind and you get them up there.

Question: Let's go back now and look at these three pages to see if your writing changed.

Child (*looking at the earliest example*): Here the writing kind of jumps around.

Question: What do you mean by "jumps around"?

Child: Sometimes the sentences don't match. Like the dog being brown and that I like to play ball. These don't really go together because the dog doesn't play ball.

Question: Let's look at this one next. Here you are writing about going to the park with your aunt.

Child: This one is better. The whole thing is about my aunt and the park and there is what we were calling *voice*—like someone is talking—you know, their voice.

Question: So there is more voice in this one. How about this writing and illustration you did last week? What do you think about this?

Child: This one has lots of talking voice. See, the wind even says *shwooooo*. Remember, I told you that my dad and I are on the sidewalk and the kite is in the sky. When I was five, I would've made me and my dad flying up there with the kite—like this first one. See, there I am with our dog in the air.

In this conference not only was the child able to recognize her progress as shown in her writing and illustrating, but she also had the vocabulary to explain her new understandings, such as the use of voice in her writing and the importance of anchoring figures to a baseline in her drawing. Her kindergarten teacher had effectively conveyed the process of communicating through illustrations and writing, helping the children develop skills in both and the vocabulary to describe the concepts they were working with.

Recording Observations of Student Teachers

Many classroom teachers will have prospective teachers in their classrooms from time to time. Observing student teachers is a good way to gain insight into the teaching process in general and to gain perspective on one's own classroom. Erica and Deyonne are practicum students in a combination classroom of first- and second-graders. To record the students' progress, the classroom teacher enters her observations in a journal as she watches them present a lesson to children on the illustration process:

Observation, Literature/Art Lesson, April 17

The children came inside from recess and sat in front of the rocking chair. Within a few minutes they were calm, attentive, and waiting for the lesson to begin. Deyonne asked them if they had read any books by Leo Lionni and showed them several books he had written. She then read Lionni's book *Swimmy* to the children.

Deyonne talked with the children about the story and then discussed how the pictures were made with paint and the fish were prints made with stamps. Erica had the children gather around one table to watch her demonstrate painting and printing techniques. She organized them, with some sitting and some standing behind the chairs. When the children were all listening, she showed them several techniques for printing and painting, including watercolors and crayon resist. After making sure all the children understood the assignment, she distributed blank booklets prepared in advance by the teacher, guided children through describing a main idea from *Swimmy* on each page, and sent the children to their tables to paint. She modeled how to remain calm when she got red paint on her white outfit, so children who got paint on themselves would not be upset. Unexpected problems developed during the painting, such as one child painting his booklet cover so thoroughly it disintegrated and another child painting over all the words on one page. Deyonne dealt with each crisis calmly. She bent down to the level of the child and helped "problem solve" a solution, such as a new cover for the booklet.

Both Deyonne and Erica circulated during the lesson and quietly interacted with children, asking them about their work. They made suggestions during the project. The teachers had a good plan for cleaning up, one table at a time. They gave each table a large cup for paintbrushes, then asked for a few volunteers to scrub the tables. Deyonne supervised this while Erica gathered the rest of the children by the rocking chair and answered questions.

After the lesson, Deyonne and Erica brainstormed things they would do differently next time. Deyonne said she would have the children read each page before painting it; Erica said she would emphasize that "You don't need a lot of paint to make a great illustration!"

This was a successful team-taught lesson. Tomorrow the children will complete the booklets by sponge printing fish onto the backgrounds. The pictures from their booklets will be mounted on the bulletin board.

A display of children's illustrations for the story Swimmy.

Working and thinking together about the creative process helps children better understand our "neighbors" in the classroom. When teachers respect children and their learning, they truly work with them to achieve new understandings. Teachers enter the classroom neighborhood and become learners along with the children. Helping children think through their illustration and writing gives them insights and greater ability to make meaning, which they continually build upon each time they illustrate their writing.

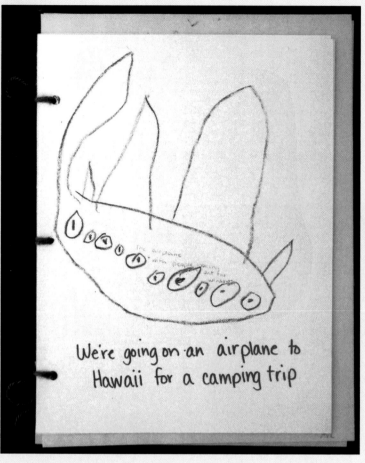

We're going on an airplane to Hawaii for a camping trip

I.GOT.TO FEED BABY GOATS!

Markers and crayons are good basic tools to begin the illustration process. In the first illustration, a four-year-old child has dictated the story to the teacher. In the second, a seven-year-old child has provided both image and text.

As children explore the illustrating process, they enjoy
experimenting with other techniques such as watercolor, sponge
painting, and fabric collage. The watercolor snowman was done by
a five-year-old child, while the sponge-painted snowwoman was
painted by a six-year-old.

This eight-year-old's fabric collage presents a wolf in a mountain scene.

This detailed collage and marker illustration was done by kindergartners and first-graders in response to reading the book The Cowboy and the Black-Eyed Pea.

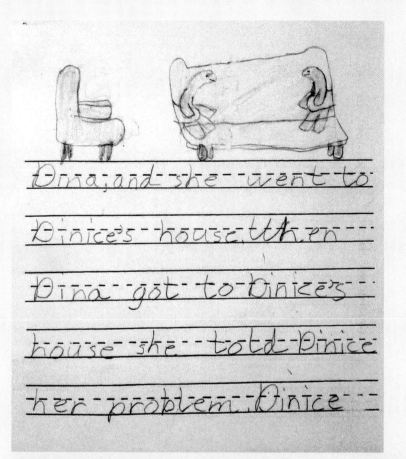

Dina, and she went to
Dinice's house, then
Dina got to Dinice's
house she told Dinice
her problem. Dinice

When children craft their own stories and illustrations they benefit from revisiting and revising their work. The image and text on the bottom of this page is a later version of the above. Both were done by the same seven-year-old child.

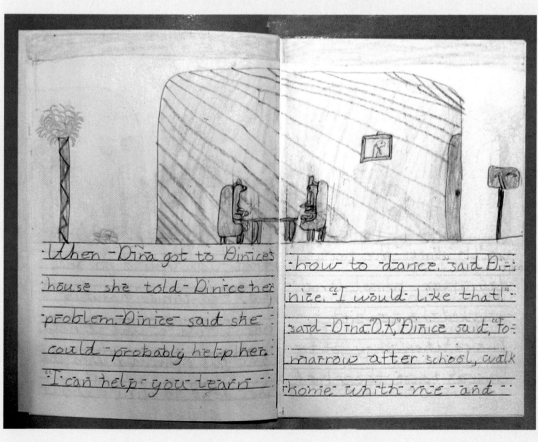

When Dina got to Dinice's
house she told Dinice her
problem. Dinice said she
could probably help her.
"I can help you learn

how to dance," said Di-
nice. "I would like that!"
said Dina. "OK," Dinice said, "to-
marrow after school, walk
home whith me and

They found the purple pebble in
and took it to the lizard. They
up mice. The lizard said, "Your v

First and second grade children collaborated on the text and illustration in this detailed collage.

the sand. They picked up the pebble
wished they could both be wind
ish is granted." The End

Children can achieve great expressive subtlety and success in their illustration and writing. In this top example, an eight-year-old's delicate oil pastel illustration sets the scene and visually conveys information. In the other, a seven-year-old has combined a title, illustration, and text to form a cohesive whole that informs the reader.

The Whooping crane

Its feathers are white. They have a wing spand of 7 feet. It can fly as fast as 40 miles per hour and is 1.5 met tall. It is the tallest bird in North America.
The head is covered with red skin.
they build nests in tall plants. The beak is pointed.
It lives in north america. They go to the Platte River in winter.

Illustration Techniques and Activities

On one of my classroom visits, I demonstrate a variety of techniques for illustrating stories using prints, and then guide the children through the process of experimenting with various printmaking techniques. By the time each child has explored several illustration techniques and completed several illustrations for stories yet to be written, our time is at an end, sooner than any of us would have liked. As we are talking about how to carefully carry prints still wet with paint, one little girl exclaims, "I had so much fun! And I thought all we were going to do was learn how to illustrate books!" Through discussion with this young girl it becomes apparent that she connects illustrations solely with drawing, completely unaware of and having no experience with other illustration techniques.

The most basic illustration method for young children is drawing, which is usually children's first form of written communication. (For more on drawing, see Chapter 2.) But children benefit from being intentionally introduced to a variety of others.

It's not enough to make an assortment of tools and materials available. To fully appreciate all the illustration possibilities, young children need us to show them examples of painting, printing, collage, rubbings, photography, sandpainting, papermaking, and all the rest. They need to examine, even play with, materials that are new to them. They need us to explain, perhaps demonstrate, a technique's steps, and to give them space and time for experimentation and practice. And they need us to help them connect what they see to their everyday experiences. Only then can they make a technique their own, and add it to their illustration repertoire.

Contents

In her lively kindergarten classroom, Kathleen creates a splatter painting by running her finger over the bristles of a toothbrush. As red paint splatters softly onto her paper, she connects what she is seeing to prior knowledge and exclaims, "Just like when it rains!" Next to her on the table are books, provided by her teacher, whose illustrators have used the splattered paint technique. Kathleen's favorite is *Monster Mama*, illustrated by Stephen Gammel, because of what she calls "haggy paint drippings."

Children enjoy exploring and learning about a variety of art materials and techniques. When they have had experiences with many different illustration techniques, they will be able to select the ones that they feel best fit their writings. Teachers can put the art materials for particular techniques in drawers labeled with both words and pictures; children can then easily find materials and tools to use in creating beautiful illustrations for their stories and poems.

About this chapter

Young children impress us with their wonderful imaginations and ability to see the limitless potential in everyday objects to become tools and toys. A wooden spoon mixes a large batch of "pancake" dough in the bathtub, a miniature marshmallow becomes a pillow for a crayon doll, and a clothespin opens and closes its "dragon mouth" at the door of the castle made from stacked spools of thread and cans of soup.

The illustration techniques in this chapter build foundational knowledge for children. With encouragement and opportunities, children will incorporate their own creative and unique ideas for using materials.

The activities each begin with a list of the materials you will need. Ask children and families to help supply materials whenever possible. Judge for yourself how many of a given item is necessary in your classroom. For example, for some activities it is optimum for every child to have a paintbrush, but children can share paints and containers of water for cleaning brushes. Always have a supply of scrap paper or newsprint handy for practice purposes.

Materials listed in brackets at the top of a materials list, such as [sharp knife] or [scissors], are for teacher use in preparation, not children's use.

The questions in the "Exploring with Children" sections are to be asked while children are working, and no response is really expected. This is why so many of them can be answered with yes or no. The nature of the questions is to raise issues that children may not have thought about that might prompt them to think in new ways or try new ideas.

Children as Illustrators

Rosy went to California. She saw a kitten
that looked like Stripey. Rosy asked the kitten
"Are you my kitten?" The kitten said "No, I am not
your kitten."

Rosy, a kindergarten child, used several different techniques to illustrate each page of her story. She used watercolors and texture rubbings, printed with paper towels, tried paper collage, and drew with markers and crayons.

Printing

Ask children if they have ever kissed a mirror and left the image of their lips on the glass. If they've done this, they've made a print!

Basically, *printing* describes the process of making an impression of an object. In the kissing example, it's the natural oils from the children's lips that make the impression on the surface of the mirror. In the classroom, printing more typically means making an impression, usually on paper, by coating the surface of an object with paint and then pressing (or "stamping") that object (or "stamp") onto the paper.

Children can think about other ways they have made prints at home or outdoors. Leaving a muddy or wet footprint on the sidewalk or on Mom's clean kitchen floor is another good example. Discuss how, throughout history, printing has been used for many interesting purposes. For example, since ancient times letters and other correspondence were sealed with melted wax and then individualized by pressing a stamp into the hot wax. Before the printing press was invented, newspapers were printed by hand with ink and small stamps. A good modern example is the stamp a librarian uses to mark the date a book is due.

Children can make prints by stamping on paper or fabric with an object that has been dipped in paint, pressed onto a stamp pad loaded with paint or ink, or painted with a design. The object might be a carved shape or it might be a leaf, a sponge, a gadget, or any number of other imaginative found materials, as you will see in the printmaking techniques that follow. When the painted surface of the stamp is pressed against the paper, the paint is transferred to the paper, and *voila!* You have a print.

When first describing the printmaking process to children, help them to understand that printed shapes do not have the clean lines that shapes painted with a brush do. Explain that their prints might seem a little blurry, but that the blurriness is part of the charm of this technique. And show them how to use a stamp correctly—first pressing it firmly but carefully against the paper and then lifting it straight up off the paper—so the paint doesn't smear.

Encourage children to practice a new printing method several times until they get a feel for the technique and how much paint to use, and an idea of how they want their print to look. Have available an abundant supply of newsprint or scrap paper for practice purposes, several colors

Original Stamp Pads

Rather than buy a supply of inked stamp pads, you and the children can make stamp pads yourselves—by rubbing tempera paint into a damp sponge. Any size sponge will work. You can vary the sponge size depending on the size of the object you are using as your stamp.

Preparing to stamp

To make a stamp pad of your own, place a damp sponge in a shallow dish or plate. Pour enough paint on the sponge so that, when rubbed in, the paint saturates the sponge. You can use a plastic spoon to rub the paint into the sponge. To keep the sponge from drying out between uses, keep the sponge in a container with a lid, or wrap the sponge in plastic. If the sponge does dry out, just clean the sponge with water, and start over with fresh paint.

As children use the pad in their printmaking, the paint on the surface of the sponge will begin to get used up. Periodically push the plastic spoon onto the top of the sponge, which will squeeze more paint to the surface. If the paint in the sponge begins to run out, simply pour a little more paint onto the sponge and press in with the spoon.

Sharing stamp pads among children is like sharing paints. It is best to have a set of stamp pads in each color for each group of children. Children can take turns using the stamps.

Practicing their skills

It's important that children learn proper stamp pad technique or they will be frustrated by the quality and inconsistency of their results. When they load their stamp with paint, for example, they need enough paint to make a good print but not so much that excess paint goes where they don't want it to on the paper. Finding just how much is just right might take some experimentation.

Once they load paint on their stamp, children need to practice pressing their stamp onto the paper cleanly, then lifting it off cleanly too, so the paint doesn't smear on the paper. This may take some practice as well. It's best to remind children about this a few times when doing a printing activity.

It's not necessary for children to renew the paint on the stamp each time they make an impression. Rather, they can make a number of impressions until the print becomes too light; then it's time for more paint.

of paint, and a small container of water in which they can wash the stamp when changing colors.

Children might already own a set of stamps with the alphabet or a theme such as dinosaurs or planets and space travel. If possible, have a few stamps and an ink pad available for children to examine and try out. This will help them understand the printing process before they begin making stamps of their own.

Older children [six to eight] making books may want to use a printmaking technique, instead of hand lettering, to put text on their book covers and inside pages. Help them understand that if they carve or paint letters onto their stamp oriented normally, that is, reading left to right and facing right, the letters in their print will come out facing backwards. Explain that they need to form the letters on the stamp backwards, that is, reading right to left and facing left—a mirror image of what is desired. This is a universal principle of printmaking, not just for lettering: All prints are a reverse of the image of the object used to make the impression.

The following printmaking techniques can work well for all children. In the directions for some techniques are adaptations for children of different developmental abilities and ages.

The printing methods in this book use many ordinary, easily obtained objects, such as polystyrene foam trays, potatoes, pieces of wood, and found materials from leaves to keys. In many cases, part of the fun of the technique for children is helping to collect the objects. Or bringing them from home.

Potato Prints

[sharp knife to cut the potatoes]
potatoes
plastic knives
pencils
stamp pads, loaded with tempera
*   paints in various colors*
water to rinse stamps
paper

French fries are not the only fun use for a potato. . . . Try a potato print!

Preparing: The potatoes probably need to be washed first. Then cut enough potatoes to provide each child with a half. Cut the potatoes in half widthwise, so children can hold onto them more easily. Be sure that the cut surface of the potato is completely flat; if it is uneven, when the child makes a print, part of the design will not appear on the paper. Prepare stamp pads, or add the making of the stamp pads to the activity.

Guiding the Activity: Let children feel the texture of the potatoes and examine them closely—even count their eyes! Children will be amazed to learn that there are thousands of varieties of potatoes in the world, not just the few typically available in their neighborhood grocery. Two good books for children about potatoes are *More Potatoes!* by Millicent E. Selsam, which explores the journey of a potato from the farm to the table, and Milton Meltzer's *The Amazing Potato: A Story in Which the Incas, Conquistadors, Marie Antoinette, Thomas Jefferson, Wars, Famines, Immigrants, and French Fries All Play a Part*, which discusses the history of the potato.

To introduce potato printing as an illustration technique, read children the book *One Potato: A Counting Book of Potato Prints*, by Diana Pomeroy. This book is a great example of illustrations done using potatoes for printing. You can also show children the cover of *Elizabeti's Doll*, by Stephanie Stuve-Boden. Although illustrator Christy Hale may not have used potatoes to make the print on this cover, explain to children that they can make a similar-looking print by using a potato as a tool.

Demonstrate making a potato print for the children: Use a pencil to draw a simple shape on the cut surface of your potato half. With a plastic knife, trim away the potato from around the pencil drawing, leaving a flat, raised area to receive the paint. This is the potato stamp.

Press the potato stamp onto a stamp pad. Then carefully press the stamp onto a piece of paper, and lift it off carefully too, so the imprint doesn't smear. Explain to children that they can repeat the process as many times as it takes to form a pattern or make a design, going back to the stamp pad for more paint when the image becomes too light.

Respect for Food

Food is expensive, and using perfectly good potatoes for an art activity can seem wasteful. It can even feel unethical or disrespectful to families whose cultures value food as a spiritual gift.

You may be able to allay such concerns by substituting discarded fruits and vegetables available from a grocery store or donated by children's families.

Now it's the children's turn. Have them draw a design of their own on the cut surface of their potato then trim away the potato from around their design with a plastic knife. They can practice printing with their potato stamp on newsprint or other practice paper until they determine how much paint they need to load and can press the potato's surface flat against the paper and lift it away without smearing the paint.

Remind children that one load of paint can make several impressions. When their images begin to get light, they can return to the stamp pad to add fresh paint. They may also need to be reminded to wash their stamp before changing colors.

Exploring with Children: "Can you lift the potato stamp straight off the paper carefully so the print does not smear?" "Does it help to have a friend hold down the edges of your paper while you lift the stamp off the paper?" "How might you use the dark images (when the stamp is loaded with paint) and the light images (when the paint is almost used up) to make patterns?"

Variation: Let the children try printing with other natural materials in addition to a potato. For example, they might create an illustration of a person with a potato print body, celery print legs and arms, and an onion print head (like the example below).

Weather Stripping Prints

[sharp scissors or mat knife]
foam rubber weather stripping
child-safe scissors
cardboard or card stock
tempera paints
paintbrushes
water to rinse paintbrushes
paper

Foam weather stripping makes a wonderful material for printmaking!

The type of weather stripping to use is foam rubber with a sticky back. It comes in rolls of various widths and can be purchased in discount or hardware stores. It is usually used to block drafts around doors and windows. Weather stripping is a great print-making material because it is easy to cut into interesting shapes and already has adhesive on one side. The adhesive allows children to easily stick their cut shape onto a piece of cardboard to make a stamp.

Preparing: Cut the weather stripping into pieces about 6 inches long for each child. Cut cardboard or stiff card stock into pieces about 2 x 4 inches each for each child.

Guiding the Activity: Discuss with children the different uses of weather stripping. Involve them in brainstorming where in a house someone might put weather stripping. For example, uses might include gaskets of various kinds—on refrigerator doors to keep cold air in and warm air out, washing machine lids to keep water in, and head gaskets in car engines to keep oil from leaking.

Talk with children about different possibilities for the shape of their stamp. Because the weather stripping is narrow, their shape must be small and simple—for example, a geometric shape or a leaf.

Show children the illustrations of the bricks in the wall in *Whistle for Willie,* by Ezra Jack Keats. These prints are a great example of the shape and kind of prints children can make with a weather stripping stamp.

Have children cut out their stamp shape using scissors. Next, they remove the backing from the adhesive and attach their shape to a piece of cardboard. This is their stamp. Finally, they carefully brush paint over the shape they cut out, and press the stamp to paper.

How much paint to put on the stamp will require some experimentation. The paint should cover the flat surface of their stamp; but if the paint is applied too liberally and is running off the surface, the print will smear. As always with a stamp, children must press and lift their stamp straight onto and up off the paper for best results. After stamping several designs, the print will become too light, and the children will need to apply more paint.

Exploring with Children: "Can you make an illustration by putting prints of different shapes together on the same piece of paper?" "Do you think prints from weather stripping would make good borders?"

Comment: Because weather stripping is narrow, it may be easier for younger children to just cut the weather stripping crosswise into short rectangles (rather than into shapes), which requires minimal use of the scissors. Older children who handle scissors better can cut out specific shapes.

Meat Tray Prints

[sharp scissors]
polystyrene foam trays
pencils
tempera paints

paintbrushes
water to rinse trays
paper

Prints created with polystyrene foam trays have the sophisticated look of wood or linoleum block prints, but the process is safe and manageable for young children.

In many grocery stores or supermarkets, meat and sometimes produce are packaged on polystyrene foam trays wrapped in plastic wrap. Because used meat trays can carry bacteria left over from the raw meat, it is safest to use new trays. Many times the stores will donate new, unused trays for children to use for art purposes. If, however, you use trays that are recycled, be sure to wash them long and well in hot water with dish detergent.

Preparing: Cut away the curved outside lip of each tray so children will have a flat piece of foam with which to work, then cut each tray into pieces. Some children may prefer to work with a small piece of foam and others will want a larger piece. Some trays have a company name or logo impressed in their middle. When you cut the trays into pieces, discard any design portions.

Guiding the Activity: Show children a reproduction of a Japanese woodblock print such as "The Great Wave," by Katsushika Hokusai, or a book such as *The Man Who Planted Trees,* by Jean Giono, which is illustrated with woodblock prints by Michael McCurdy. Explain that the artists carved their designs into blocks of wood and then used ink to print them on paper.

Explain to children that they can make a print that looks somewhat like a woodblock print by using a similar process—scratching a design in the tray, applying paint to the surface, and carefully stamping their design on paper.

Have the children scratch a design into their foam piece using a pencil or the tip of a paintbrush handle. Next, with their foam piece laying flat on the table, face up, they use a paintbrush to put a thin, even coat of paint over the entire face of the foam, coating the unscratched (raised) areas of the tray. The scratched design should stay white and be free of paint. Children print their design by carefully laying a piece of paper over the tray, gently rubbing across the surface of the paper with their hands, and then peeling the paper carefully away.

The trays can be washed off when children are ready to change colors of paint for a new print.

Exploring with Children: "Is your print sharper if you use a lot of paint on your design or not as much paint?" "Could you imprint the title of your book into your tray? When you print a word this way, does it print backwards? If so, what can you do so it prints forward?"

Comment: When the paper is lifted off of the tray, the print should have a clear design; the design will be smeared if the paint was applied too thickly. If this happens, encourage the young artist to make another print with a fresh piece of paper without adding any more paint. Also, if children allow the paint to seep into the scratched areas, their design won't show up on the paper; instead they will get just a solid painted area on the paper.

Gadget Prints

*assortment of small gadgets collected
by children
tempera paints, in paper plates
or shallow dishes
water to rinse gadgets
paper*

Exciting prints can be made from those odds
and ends found around children's homes or
the classroom.

Preparing: Involve children in collecting an
assortment of odds and ends that have interesting shapes. These might include spools,
small toys, buttons, kitchen gadgets, knobs,
keys, small brushes, and chains.

Guiding the Activity: Let children examine
the objects, discuss the different shapes, and
sort and classify them by attributes such as
shape, color, and texture. Then involve them
in experimenting with printmaking using
these gizmos and gadgets.

For example, children can dip a piece of
string into the paint and drop, drag, or roll it
on a sheet of paper. Or they might stamp a
gadget onto the paper. Encourage them to
experiment with a variety of objects to create a
richly textured composition.

Exploring with Children: "Does the gadget
make the design you thought it would?" "Can
you make a pattern with your gadget?"
"Looking at your neighbor's print, can you
guess what gadget he or she has used to make
it?"

Leaf (and Other Natural Materials) Prints

[sharp scissors or rotary cutter]
assortment of natural materials collected by children
tempera paints
paintbrushes
water to rinse paintbrushes
paper or cloth

Some of the nicest prints can be made using natural materials from a child's yard or a nearby park.

Preparing: Explain to the children that a "natural" material is one that occurs in nature and is not manufactured by humans. Have them brainstorm natural materials, such as cornhusks, apples, bark, and leaves. Take them outdoors on a natural materials hunt. Young children will enjoy carrying a bag and pretending they are birds looking for materials to build a nest. Children can collect

leaves, twigs, bark, and such. You might want to supply cornhusks and other natural materials that the children are unlikely to find.

Leaves make especially beautiful prints on white cloth, so you may want to substitute pieces of cloth for paper. You might offer red, orange, yellow, and brown paints to give leaf prints a fall look.

If you plan to use cloth instead of paper, cut the cloth into pieces about one foot square.

Guiding the Activity: Share Lois Ehlert's book *Red Leaf, Yellow Leaf* with the children. Guide them in examining the illustrations and talk with children about how they will be using their natural materials to make similar prints. Encourage children to carefully examine their natural materials. Talk about the textures they feel and what they can observe about the materials.

Suggest that they might sort them, and discuss different classifications. Children may well be very interested in identifying which trees the different leaves they collect come from. A good book that shows leaf collages children can make and identifies leaf variations is *Look What I Did with a Leaf,* by Morteza E. Sohi.

Have children select an item to work with, then brush paint on the part of it they want to print with. They can use several different materials in each print.

Exploring with Children: "What kinds of patterns can you see in your natural materials prints?" "Do these patterns look like the textures of the materials that made them? How are your prints similar?" "Does one side of the natural material print more clearly than the other side?"

Variation: Images of leaves and other natural materials can be permanently printed onto white T-shirts if you use acrylic paint instead of tempera. After the imprints dry, turn the T-shirts inside out and press the images on the wrong side of the fabric with a warm iron. This sets the paints so they will not bleed or fade when the shirt is washed. A printed shirt becomes not only an illustration but also a great conversation piece.

What's "Natural"?

I like to talk with children to hear their ideas about natural materials.

I once conducted a workshop with children, involving them in different activities. Some were making impressions in clay using shells, others were printing with fruits and vegetables, and some were using potatoes to make potato-head people. While they were working, I talked with them about the materials they were using.

A child of about 8, working with clay, turned to me and said, "Actually, everything comes from natural materials because you can't just make something from nothing!"

Monoprints

thick paints, such as finger paints or
   thick tempera paints

paintbrushes

smooth surface(s) to paint on

water to rinse surface(s)

sponges

paper

Monoprinting is different from other printing techniques that allow children to make multiple prints from the same object. Children can create only one print during the monoprint process. Monoprints can be made using any smooth surface. Mirrors, plastic laminate or metal tabletops, and glass windowpanes work well, for example.

Preparing: Place a mirror or other flat, smooth-surfaced object on the work table. Only one child at a time can do a monoprint unless you provide more than one printing surface.

Guiding the Activity: Demonstrate the technique for the children first. To make a monoprint, paint a design on the smooth surface, then lay a piece of paper on top of the painted design. Rub the paper gently with your hand, and peel off the paper to reveal your print. Last, sponge any remaining paint off the surface, so it is clean and ready for the next artist to use. Now it's the children's turn.

In monoprinting, a child who paints the outline of a tree on the surface, for example, may be pleased and surprised to see that the print looks like the design that was painted, only the lines will be wider because of the spreading paint. The paint will spread less if less paint is used.

You may have to remind children that they must always clean the surface after making a print.

Exploring with Children: "Does the paint spread more if you use a bigger brush? Why or why not?" "Does your print look different if you try different amounts of paint?"

Variation 1: Instead of using a brush to paint their design on the surface, children can apply the paint on the surface broadly, then use their hands and fingers to create their design before printing. Or instead of using their hands and fingers, they can use a Popsicle stick to scratch a design in the paint before printing.

Variation 2: *Gyotaku* ("fish rubbing") has its roots in early 19th-century Japan, where monoprinting the fish they caught was a way for fishermen to measure and record the size of their catch. Children may enjoy the novelty of a print using a fish. Plastic, rubber, or real fish can be used. In this technique, the fish takes the place of the smooth surface. A real fish will be difficult or impossible to clean of paint, and so is useable only once.

Comment: Beware that in some cultures or for some families, using a real fish may send a message of disrespect for the valuable purpose of food.

Children as Illustrators

Sponge Prints

[sharp scissors]
damp sponges
child-safe scissors
tempera paints, in paper plates or shallow dishes
paper

Printing with pieces of sponges can make wonderful backgrounds, add texture to a drawing, and make interesting borders or figures. Large kitchen sponges work well.

Preparing: Cut each sponge in half widthwise and cut each half into three long strips. Wet the sponges and wring them out so they are damp, before giving them to children to use. Have enough sponges available so there is one sponge piece per color of paint.

Guiding the Activity: Show the children the book *The Mud Pony*, by Caron Lee Cohen. Tell the children they can use sponges to get an effect similar to its illustrations by Shonto Begay. Children can use the sponge pieces whole, cut them into smaller sections, or trim them into interesting shapes. Damp sponges are easily cut with scissors.

Once the children have the size and shape they want, have them dip the surface of their sponge piece into the paint (it doesn't take much). They should practice printing on a piece of scrap paper or a paper towel until they feel comfortable with the amount of paint to apply and are happy with the resulting print.

If children are using the sponge to produce a shape, they must place the sponge on the paper and then carefully lift it straight up or the print will smear. Warn children not to press too hard, or they may lose detail.

If children use a sponge piece to create texture within a shape, such as fur on a bear, or to make a textured background, they need not be so precise. They just dip the sponge in the paint and print onto the paper over and over, refilling with paint, until the impressions fill the desired area.

Exploring with Children: "Does the sponge make a background that looks like grass, mountains, or the sky?" "What other materials can you dip into paint to make a similar texture?" "Do you think a crumpled paper towel would make an interesting background or texture print? What else besides a sponge or paper towel would you like to try?"

Clay Stamp Prints

clay (any kind will do)
pencils
tempera paints
paintbrushes
water to rinse paintbrushes
paper

Clay is easy to pinch into shapes to make small stamps for printing.

Preparing: Make a small, one-inch ball of clay for each child.

Guiding the Activity: Explain to children that they are going to make stamps from the small pieces of clay, and that clay stamps are especially good for making borders and for lettering. Clay stamps are easy for children to stamp a repeated design around the edge or carefully stamp letters evenly spaced and in line for a book title. Children will enjoy seeing how Eric Carle used similar stamps to print an entire inside cover for his book *Rooster's Off to See the World.*

First, demonstrate how to pinch a ball of clay to make a stamp for printing. Use your fingers in a pinching motion to mold the clay into a thick tubular shape, then press the end of the shape on the table until the end is flat. It is on this flat surface that children scratch their design.

Next explain and demonstrate how they will use a pencil to scratch a design into the flat surface of their clay stamp. The scratched design will be the portion that doesn't take the paint. Finally, brush paint over the stamp and print the design on paper. Now it's the children's turn.

One nice thing about clay stamps is that if children don't like the results, they can pinch off the end of their stamp and reform the flat surface to create a new stamp.

Exploring with Children: "Would you like to try printing an entire page with a design that fits your story, like Eric Carle did on the inside cover of *Rooster's Off to See the World*?" "Can you make a few clay stamps, scratch letters into them, and stamp out the title to your book? Look at your title; how many letters will you have to make?" "If you had to print your entire book with clay stamps, would it be harder than writing your story with a pencil or typing it on a computer?"

Variation: Rather than scratching a design of their own, children can create interesting stamp designs with textures collected from their environment. They simply press the flat surface of their clay stamp onto a textured surface, such as tree bark, a brick, or the tread of a bike tire. These stamps make great borders to frame artwork or a story!

Wood Piece Prints

pieces of wood, in different sizes and shapes
sandpaper
stamp pads loaded with tempera paints
water to rinse wood pieces
paper

Pieces of wood help keep children connected to the outdoors, and the wood grains are intriguingly unique.

Preparing: Collect many small pieces of wood in different shapes. If possible, include children in collecting the wood from fallen trees or branches, discard piles at lumber stores, or scraps from someone children know who works with wood.

Guiding the Activity: To help them gain an appreciation of this interesting natural material, read children the book *Wood*, by Christin Ditchfield, and discuss with them the different types of wood such as oak, pine, and fir. Additional wood activities can expand their understanding and make connections to science and the natural world (see box).

Explain that pieces of wood make interesting printmaking tools because of the wide variety of shapes the wood pieces make without having to carve or otherwise alter them. While the children observe, demonstrate this print technique—basically pressing a piece of wood or a piece of a branch onto the stamp pad, then pressing the wood onto a piece of paper to make a print. The wood can be washed off and used again with a different color.

Exploring with Children: "Did you use blocks of different shapes in your illustration?" "Did you try printing one color onto part of another color?" "What kind of tree did your piece of wood come from?"

(continued on p. 94)

The Wonders of Wood

There is much to appreciate about wood, and this topic could be the basis for a class project on wood or trees.

Guide children to research and identify types of wood themselves—have books available and wood samples. Include pieces of wood and bark from a range of species such as cherry, oak, maple, and pine. Samples from nature can be found outdoors; milled samples of many woods used in homebuilding and hobby projects can be purchased in a lumber store. (Pressure-treated wood should not be used with children as it can contain toxic chemicals.)

Involve the children in carefully observing each piece of wood. What do they observe about its texture, color, and smell? Are there similarities among the pieces? Differences? Provide materials so children can sand the pieces of wood, feeling the smooth and rough textures, and observing their color.

Children can explore the science concept of *density* by holding a piece of wood in each hand and feeling which piece might be heavier. The pieces of wood will need to be about the same size. Suggest children order the various woods, from the heaviest to the lightest. Use a balance scale to check the results.

Different woods have very distinct odors. The children can smell the wood pieces and compare and contrast their different odors. If the children get the wood wet, often the smells will be stronger.

All coniferous trees (trees with leaves that look like needles) are "softwoods." Deciduous trees (trees with broad, flat leaves that drop) are "hardwoods." Make available a variety of branches. Have the children group the branches according to their leaf type, at the same time identifying them to be hardwood or softwood. After the children have classified the branches, talk about the similarities and differences between the two kinds of wood. For example, with older children provide materials so they can hammer large tacks into various woods, experimenting with wood that is hard and wood that is soft.

As a group, discuss and record the children's observations.

Variation: Children can try painting on wood to experiment with painting on a surface other than paper or fabric. Stefano Vitale painted intricate designs and scenes on pieces of wood to create illustrations and borders in Judy Sierra's book *Nursery Tales Around the World.*

Comment: Do not allow children to handle lumber that has been chemically treated for exterior use; certain chemical treatments may be toxic.

Children as Illustrators

Painting

Talk with children about painting they have done—all kinds of painting. Children may have helped to paint a wall at home, painted at an easel at school, or even painted a piece of furniture. As children talk about their different painting experiences, help them think about the kinds of paints they were using. For example, paint for interior walls is probably latex acrylic, whereas easel paint is probably tempera paint or maybe watercolor. Was the paint thick or watery? Did it come in a jar, a big can, or a tube? Did they need to add water? How did children apply the paint? They may have used paintbrushes, a roller, or even sponges.

Many children's book illustrators use paints to create illustrations. Their techniques include everything from paintbrush and watercolors to blowing paint and splattering paint with a toothbrush. These and many other creative, imaginative techniques are detailed in the painting activities that follow. Encourage children to try a variety of methods as well as different kinds of paints and textures of paper.

Paint Blowing

[sharp scissors]
drinking straws
tempera paints, thinned with water, in cups
plastic spoons
paper

Blown paint can look drippy, shaggy, and imaginative!

Preparing: Cut the drinking straws in half—shorter straws give children better control when they are blowing paint. Each child will need to start with a clean straw each time and then throw it away when the activity is over, to avoid spreading germs.

Mix a small amount of water into the paint so that it blows more easily, but not too much. Too much water makes the paint too thin, and it will not show up very well on the paper.

Guiding the Activity: In the book *Monster Mama*, by Liz Rosenberg, illustrator Stephen Gammell creates illustrations by blowing, dripping, and splattering paint. His unusual techniques will inspire children to try blowing paint to make illustrations of their own.

Demonstrate paint blowing first. Place about one-half a spoonful of paint in the middle of a sheet of paper. Hold the straw about an inch from the paper and point it at the center of the puddle. Blow through the straw hard enough to move the paint across the paper, but not so hard that the paint sprays wildly.

Caution children not to suck on the straw or they may get paint in their mouth. Children younger than four may not have the control needed for this activity.

Now it's the children's turn. First, they spoon paint onto their paper. Then, holding the straw close to the paint, they blow the paint into designs. Remind children that they need to hold their straws only about an inch from the paper; show them again how close that is.

Children can spoon on more paint and other colors to other areas of the paper and blow some more. After they have had a chance to experiment with blowing into the middle of a puddle of paint, suggest that they try blowing the puddle of paint from one side or another instead of in the middle, creating a more controlled, less random design.

Exploring with Children: "What does your design remind you of? Could it be an animal, a tree, or a cloud?" "Does it help to turn your paper while you are blowing?"

Variation: After children have finished blowing the paint into a design and the paint has dried, they can use crayons or markers to add details.

Comment: Watch for children who feel lightheaded from blowing. Have them sit down and rest, breathing deeply, until the dizziness passes.

Children as Illustrators

Splatter Painting

newspaper

shallow boxes or other containers

tempera paints, in cups or dishes

toothbrushes

water to rinse toothbrushes

paper

This technique creates interesting splatters of paint, and it's fun!

Preparing: This technique can be messy—the paint tends to splatter off the paper. Use newspaper to cover the children's work tables. Paint smocks or oversized shirts from home will help keep children's clothing free of paint.

To cut down on the mess factor even more, on top of the newspapers place large, shallow boxes or plastic containers such as dishpans. If children place their paper inside a box before they start spattering, most of the stray paint will stay in the container.

Guiding the Activity: In this technique, children dip a toothbrush in paint and then flick the bristles with their finger, spattering the paint onto paper. But before they begin, children need to think about how they should hold the toothbrush to make sure the paint spatters downward, onto the paper. Caution them to hold the toothbrush bristle-side down. Ask them what would happen if they ran their finger over the paint-filled bristles with the bristles facing up.

Children can practice before they begin painting. Have them dip the bristles of the toothbrush into paint, hold the brush, bristles down, over scrap paper or newsprint, and run their finger or thumb over the bristles. When they begin to feel they can control their splatters, they can try using the technique in their own illustrations.

Talk about when splattering is effective in an illustration. Some children might say splat-

tering can represent a snow storm, others might talk about splattering paint for a background. Broach the subject of textures and mood by sharing the book *The Tiny Seed*. In that book, Eric Carle used the splatter technique to create the backgrounds. Illustrator Robert Roth adds charm to his watercolors with small, controlled splattering in Sylvia Rosa-Casanova's book *Mama Provi and the Pot of Rice*.

Exploring with Children: "As you use up the paint on your brush, what happens to the splattering dots? Do they become smaller?" "When you have more paint on your brush, are the spatters larger?" "Try using a combination of dots that use less paint and dots that use more."

Watercolors

newspaper

watercolors

paintbrushes

water to moisten paints

water to rinse paintbrushes

paper (watercolor, drawing, or other sturdy and absorbent paper)

The depth and flow of color in watercolors work to excellent effect in illustrations of landscapes, sunsets, seascapes, fields, skies, storms, and flowers, as well as in abstract designs.

Preparing: Cover the children's work tables with newspaper and place one set of watercolors in the middle of the table for every four children.

Guiding the Activity: Read aloud a book illustrated with watercolors, such as *The Legend of the Bluebonnet,* by Tomie DePaola. Ask children to describe how the illustrations look and how they make the children feel. Children may mention that they look soft, bright, or even quiet. Encourage children to look through books in the classroom and identify other illustrations done with watercolors.

Watercoloring involves dipping a brush in water, then swirling the wet brush in the pigment until the brush is loaded with paint. The less water added to the pigment, the more intense the color and more controlled the flow of wet paint onto the paper will be— and vice versa. Children who have never watercolored before will need guidance on how much water to use. You may want to demonstrate how varying the amount of water changes the way the painting turns out.

Remind them that they must thoroughly rinse their paintbrush in water before changing colors. Explain also that they cannot keep adding water to the painting, because the wet paper eventually will tear.

Children may want to begin by painting abstract designs or shapes, because watercolors bleed and details are difficult for young children to paint. After children have experimented with watercolors they might be ready to paint an illustration with details. They may want to draw an outline first with a pencil, then fill in the drawing with paint, or they might just begin painting with watercolors without drawing.

Younger children may find it easier to use watercolors for just backgrounds and then use markers or crayons to draw an illustration on the background once the paint is dry.

Exploring with Children: "What happens when the edge of one color runs into another color?" "Try using only a little water on your paint-brush when you use the paints. Is the color darker? What happens to the color when you add more water?" "What happens if you dampen your paper with a sponge or spray bottle? Does the paint run together in beautiful colors?"

Variation: Encourage children to paint their same illustration with tempera paints, then compare the two processes. Ask them to think about how the two kinds of paint look alike and how they are different. Which kind of paint is easier to control?

Children as Illustrators

Crayon Resist

crayons

watercolors

paintbrushes

water to moisten paints

water to rinse paintbrushes

paper

This is a good technique for children, because they can create an illustration using crayons, then paint over it with watercolors with seemingly magical results—a detailed illustration with a painted background.

Preparing: If children aren't already familiar with watercolors, have them experiment with that technique first (see "Watercolors" on p. 98). Be sure to remind them to always wash their brush before changing paint colors.

Guiding the Activity: While the children watch, use a crayon to draw a simple design on a sheet of white paper. Ask them what they think will happen if you were to paint over the drawing with watercolors. Some children may guess that the paint will not stick to the crayon. Paint over the crayon drawing, and talk about how clearly the crayon shows through. Explain that this technique is called *crayon resist* because the crayon is made of wax and wax resists water.

Ask them where else in the everyday world might they see wax resisting water? Children will have excellent observations, such as when we wax the car or waterproof our boots. They may relate other experiences with wax too, such as birthday candles dripping onto the cake or their clothing. Some children may remember coloring with crayons on eggs and then dipping them in dye for Easter. You may want to show children a batik textile, because the crayon resist technique is similar to one artists use to print batik fabric. Margaret Mahy's book *17 Kings and 42 Elephants* was illustrated by Patricia MacCarthy with colorful batik paintings on silk.

After they have had a chance to experiment a bit, have children use crayons to draw their illustration and then watercolor over the drawing. For a nighttime effect, children can draw with a white crayon and then paint over their drawing with black paint.

Exploring with Children: "Try writing words with a white crayon on white paper and then paint over the message—is it like drawing with invisible ink?" "Which stands out better against the paint, darker crayons or lighter crayons?"

Variation: Place a piece of wax paper over a sheet of white paper and hold it in place with paper clips. Children can scratch a picture or design into the wax paper with the end of a paintbrush handle or a Popsicle stick. This transfers the design in wax onto the paper. When the wax paper is removed and children watercolor on the white paper, the wax transferred to the paper will resist the paint and the design will remain white against a field of color. (This technique works best with second or third grade children.)

Finger Painting

large, flat container of water
spray bottles filled with water
finger paints
plastic spoons
finger painting paper

Small fingers can create swirls, loops, and zigzags!

Preparing: Smocks or old shirts can be used to cover children's clothes, as children can get quite messy during the painting.

Guiding the Activity: Explain to children that in this technique they will use their fingers and hands (instead of paintbrushes) to create wonderful illustrations! Eric Carle is a good example of an illustrator who uses finger painting for everything from backgrounds to representational images. Carle's book *Little Cloud* is a good one to share because it illustrates this technique.

Have children wet one side of their sheet of finger painting paper by dragging that side over the surface of the water in the container or by spraying it with a water bottle. You may want to monitor this task—paint will not swirl around easily if the paper is not wet enough. Once the paper is wet, children can spoon some paint onto their paper, or you can put the paint onto their paper for them.

Suggest or demonstrate how children can use their hands and fingers as tools to move the paint around on the paper, even their fist, knuckles, side of the hand, elbow, and thumb! As children paint, you or they can spray additional water on their paper to keep their paint from drying before they are finished working.

Children will soon find that when they layer one color over another, the colors mix together to form a third (sometimes muddy) color. If children want to keep the colors more separate, they can limit each color to a different area of their paper and then gently blend only the edges of the colors together. Remind children to wash their hands before touch-

ing a new color if they want to keep each color separate.

Demonstrate how paint can be removed from a painted area by gently wiping the area with a damp sponge or cloth.

Encourage children not to overwork their painting, but to stop when they have created an illustration they are happy with. When they overwork the illustration, the wet paper will begin to tear and overcombined colors will become a muddy brown.

When their paintings are finished, lay them out flat to dry on a table or on the floor in a corner of the room. Later, paintings that have curled while drying can be flattened if you press the backs of the paintings with a cool iron.

A dry finger painting can be cut into shapes, which can then be used to make a collage, like Eric Carle did in *Little Cloud*.

Exploring with Children: "Can you use your hand to make a thin stroke, a thick stroke, or a curvy design?" "How about the side of your hand? Does it work as a tool?" "What happens when you add one color on top of the other?"

Variation: Prints can be made from fresh finger paintings. Demonstrate by laying a new piece of dry, white drawing paper on top of a still-wet finger painting and gently smoothing the dry paper over the painted design. Then carefully lift the newly created print off the original finger painting.

Talk about how a print of a finger painting makes a good book cover. Because the print's paint is not thick like the paint on the original finger painting, when dried the print can be handled and folded without the paint flaking off. Like a finger painting, the print also can be pressed with a cool iron or cut into shapes.

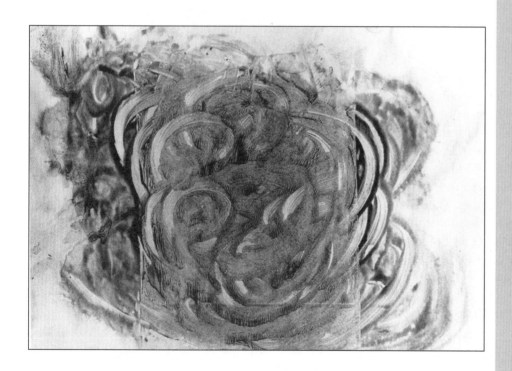

Original Finger Paint

Some children might want to make their own finger paints. Because heat is required, close supervision is necessary, especially with younger children.

1/3 cup cornstarch
3 tablespoons sugar
2 cups cold water
food coloring

In a large pan over low heat, stir together the cornstarch, sugar, and water until the mixture thickens (about five minutes). Remove from heat and divide the mixture evenly among several bowls. Add a drop or so of food coloring to each bowl of paint and mix. Let the paints cool before using them.

Pointillism

newspaper

paintbrushes or cotton-tipped swabs

tempera paints, in shallow plates or trays

water to rinse paintbrushes

paper

When a pointillist illustration is viewed from a distance, the brain blends the dots to see an image.

Preparing: A fine-tipped paintbrush provides the most control and smallest dots. Beforehand, cover the children's work table with newspaper. Children can share the paints as long as each child has a paintbrush or cotton swab for each color.

Guiding the Activity: Explain that some artists use a technique known as *pointillism,* in which thousands of small dots of color visually combine to create an entire illustration. Artists who use pointillism work very patiently and carefully.

Show children a pointillist's painting such as one by French impressionist Georges Seurat (1859–91). Have them examine it up close, then step back and look at it. Also show them a book such as *Stories to Solve: Folktales from Around the World,* by George Shannon, which has stories and poems illustrated by Peter Sis using pointillism.

Demonstrate how children will combine dots of paint to create an illustration. The dots of paint should be small and close together. Then involve children in creating their own pointillist illustrations.

Children must dip just the tip of their paintbrush in the paint, or they can dip a cotton swab or even their finger into the paint instead. By gently dabbing the paint onto their paper, they create the dots or very short strokes necessary in this technique.

Exploring with Children: "What would it be like to paint the outside of your house using pointillism? How about the wall of your room?" "Could you make an illustration with dots from a pencil?" "What happens when you use your finger as your painting tool, instead of the paintbrush or cotton swab?"

Variation 1: In this variation best used with older children, paper dots affixed with glue substitute for the painted dots. Provide a hole punch and have children punch out piles of dots from different colors of construction paper. This method is interesting and effective in terms of design; however, young children may have a hard time working with the glue and the dots, which tend to get stuck to small fingers.

Variation 2: Older children can experiment with the idea of making *secondary* colors (e.g., green) by placing dots of two *primary* colors (e.g., yellow and blue) next to each other; viewed from a distance, the two primaries will be seen as blending together. Use a color wheel to describe this concept that will allow children to make an orange sunrise, for example, from alternating dots of yellow and red.

Children as Illustrators

Fabric Painting

[sharp scissors or rotary cutter]
[masking tape]
[cardboard (optional)]
pencils
tempera or acrylic paints
paintbrushes with fine points
water to rinse paintbrushes
fabric (white or beige cotton)

Painting on fabric makes children feel very special because many children have never had an opportunity to work such material; the soft texture pleases their senses.

Preparing: Cut the fabric into pieces, each about the size of a book page. Use masking tape to tape down the edges of the fabric directly on the children's work table. Another way to prepare is to cut sheets of cardboard just larger than the fabric pieces, and tape the fabric to the cardboard instead of to the table. Taping the fabric holds it flat as children paint on it.

Guiding the Activity: Explain that all over the world, for thousands of years, people have decorated cloth with designs and pictures by painting, dyeing, and drawing on it. Sometimes the decorated fabrics tell a story. Show children pieces of fabric, such as batik, with designs or stories on them. In her book *If a Bus Could Talk: The Story of Rosa Parks*, Faith Ringgold illustrated the story by painting folk art pictures on fabric. Ringgold, a noted African American artist and storyteller, is famous not only for her children's books but also for her story quilts, which are paintings on fabric depicting stories of her childhood. The quilts are bordered by strips of muslin inscribed with that quilt's story. (A good book about Faith Ringgold's experiences growing up in Harlem is Robyn Montana Turner's *Faith Ringgold: Portraits of Women Artists for Children*.)

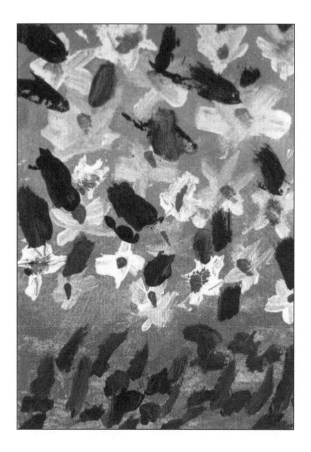

In this activity, each child tells a story of his or her own on fabric. First, have children use a pencil to lightly draw a scene depicting their story on their fabric square. Then they carefully paint in their scene, washing their brush between colors.

Exploring with Children: "Does it feel different to paint on fabric instead of paper?" "Does paint on fabric feel or look different from paint on paper?"

Variation 1: Silk paints on pieces of silk fabric can create wonderful effects. The dyes run and spread on the silk, so detailed paintings do not work well; however, large images can be striking. Silk painting is appropriate for older children.

Variation 2: Instead of creating their design using paint, children can use fabric crayons. Either they can first lightly draw the scene in pencil, or they can draw and color the scene directly with the crayons only. Ask them to think about any differences they might notice between coloring on paper with crayons and using crayons on fabric.

Variation 3: Older children may want to create a project that resembles one of Faith Ringgold's story quilts. For this project, help children glue a square piece of muslin or white cotton onto a stiff piece of paper or tag board. The paper should extend at least three inches beyond the fabric on all four sides to make a frame around the fabric. Children then paint their story on the fabric, and use pens to write their story on the paper frame. The children can then cut squares of wrapping paper, wallpaper, or even fabric and glue the squares around the very outside edges of the paper, bordering the story.

Collage

A collage is a composition that combines different objects. The objects can be any kind of paper (i.e., paper collage) but are not limited to paper. Numerous materials could be pasted, glued, stapled, or taped, usually onto a background, to make a collage. Natural materials can be used, everything from broken eggshells, corn husks, or leaves to bones, seeds, or wool. A collage could also contain other materials such as zippers, beads, ribbons, cotton balls, fabric scraps, springs, jewelry, buttons, or checkers. Materials must only be clean and have some aesthetic appeal.

Typically, materials are glued to a piece of stiff paper. But they could be attached to other things, such as cardboard, a box lid, or even an egg carton. Collecting the materials can itself be a meaningful part of the activity for children. Brainstorm with them different materials they could use in their collages to form a picture, a portrait, or a pattern or to create a mood.

Show children a variety of books with reproductions of different types of collages. *The Snowy Day,* by Ezra Jack Keats, is illustrated with collages. *Abuela,* by Arthur Dorros and illustrated by Elisa Kleven, is a joyous book about a girl and her grandmother. Available in Spanish and English, it is illustrated with multimedia collages. Jennifer L. Atkinson's resource book *Collage Art: A Step-by-Step Guide and Showcase* (1996) explores numerous types of collage possibilities.

The paper cutouts of French impressionist Henri Matisse and African American Harlem Renaissance painter Romare Bearden are also excellent examples to share with children.

If children will be using collage techniques to illustrate their books, they may not initially understand how a three-dimensional piece of artwork can become a two-dimensional illustration for a page in their story. Explain the method you will use. Collages can be photographed using a digital camera and the image printed to paper, or a conventional photo of a collage can be scanned and then printed out. If the collage itself is relatively flat, it can sometimes be scanned directly.

Children enjoy creating rich, textured collages that make their stories and poems exciting. Some children may join together to make a montage—an extended collage built around a theme, such as school or family or neighborhood, and that might include words and images (Schirrmacher 2002). A collage often will incorporate elements created using other techniques. For example, rubbings, described in the Other Techniques section beginning on p. 113, make great backgrounds for collages. Gadgets, natural materials, fabric pieces, and paper shapes can be added on top.

Paper Collage

paper (a variety of paper types, including wallpaper)
child-safe scissors
glue (sticks or bottles)
construction paper (for background)

Torn paper versus paper cut with scissors are two options, each giving a paper collage a unique texture. Even young children who cannot yet control a pair of scissors can successfully tear paper.

Preparing: To use wallpaper, ask at a local paint or decorating store for wallpaper sample books that are being discarded. Cut the pages from the sample books and spread them on a table for children's easy selection. To use magazines, look for those with age-appropriate photographs.

Guiding the Activity: Paper collages can be created with many types of paper—paper already printed with images or not, colored paper or white, wallpaper, magazine illustrations, newspaper. (See also "Tissue Paper Collage" on p. 107.)

Share books with children that have illustrations made using a paper collage technique, such as Giles Laroche's illustrations in Rachel Field's book *General Store*. In the Caldecott Honor book *There Was an Old Lady Who Swallowed a Fly*, by Simms Taback, the text is highlighted by torn paper collage. *The Little Red Hen (Makes a Pizza)*, by Philemon Sturges and illustrated by Amy Walrod, will make children laugh and is illustrated with cut paper collages.

While the children watch, demonstrate how to cut or tear pieces of paper into shapes. Explain and show children how they can better control the shape of the pieces if they tear carefully. Then have children cut or tear the paper into pieces and lay the pieces on their background paper to create an illustration. After they are happy with their arrangement of paper pieces, children can glue the pieces down.

Children can begin by experimenting with placing torn or cut pieces together and overlapping the pieces to make an abstract design. After gaining confidence and some skill, older children can try

smaller cutouts for illustration, like Laroche does in *General Store*.

Exploring with Children: "When you are tearing paper, can you control the shapes better if you tear slowly or quickly?" "Which words describe the texture of the torn edges?" "Would the wallpaper make interesting borders around your illustration?" "How about using wallpaper to make covers for your book or to line the inside of the covers of your book?"

Variation 1: Supply white construction paper, tempera paints, and paintbrushes and let children paint the white paper in colors of their choosing and creation. Once their painted papers are dry, they can proceed with their collage. Painting sheets of paper itself allows children to experiment with color and provides for a broader range of hues and tones.

Variation 2: Other materials can be easily incorporated into a paper collage. Aluminum foil can be cut into pieces and added for sparkly details, as Marcus Pfister did in *The Rainbow Fish*. Children also can add other items, maybe stick-on stars, yarn, buttons, or natural materials such as leaves.

Tissue Paper Collage

tissue paper in various colors and patterns

child-safe scissors

glue mixture (3 parts white glue, 1 part water), in small dishes

paintbrushes or small sponges

construction paper (for background)

Tissue paper makes special collages because tissue is translucent. When layered, the colors of the various paper layers show through and new colors can be made by overlapping pieces.

Preparing: Save tissue paper from the inside of store boxes, save it from presents, and buy it when it is on sale after a holiday. Spread the paper out on a table so children can easily select what colors they would like to use. Make up the glue mixture.

Guiding the Activity: Talk with children about a sunrise or sunset they have seen or a sky they noticed on a blustery day. Discuss how some artists use different techniques to capture those rich color patterns of the sky. In her book *Shadow*, Marcia Brown uses spectacular paper collages to create very rich illustrations.

Tissue paper is a very good technique for capturing some of these rich colors. Eric Carle is well known for his tissue paper collages, such as the collage illustrations in his book *Pancakes, Pancakes!* and in Bill Martin's book *Brown Bear, Brown Bear, What Do You See?* Another tissue collage example is Mem Fox's book *Hattie and the Fox*, illustrated by Patricia Mullins.

To create a landscape such as a sunrise or sunset, have children cut or tear small squares of tissue paper of different colors and arrange them, with the edges overlapping to combine the colors, on a piece of white construction paper. When they have an arrangement that pleases them, they brush the glue-and-water mixture over the layered tissue paper; the glue mixture will soak through the layers and hold everything in place. Young children who have a

difficult time manipulating a brush can dip a small, dry sponge in the glue mixture and use the sponge to dab the glue on.

Beyond creating landscapes, suggest children cut or tear various shapes from the tissue paper, perhaps combined with other materials, to create a picture. They use the same technique—painting the water-and-glue mixture over the picture as they place the different shapes on the paper. For example, overlapping long strips torn from blue and green tissue can make an effective underwater scene, with imaginary sea creatures in colorful construction paper glued on top of and under the tissue layers.

Exploring with Children: "What colors could you place together to create a sunset? How about the woods in autumn?" "How does the surface of your picture look after you have painted the glue-and-water mixture over it?"

Variation: Tissue paper collage makes a colorful background for a silhouette (again, see Marcia Brown's book *Shadow*). Explain that a silhouette is a dark shape that stands out against a lighter or different color background. Features and details of the figure cannot be seen, only its outline. Show children how to cut a simple shape such as an elephant or a tree from construction paper (silhouettes traditionally are black), brush glue on the back, and glue the shape on the collage background. Children can create entire scenes in silhouette.

Natural Materials Collage

natural materials

white glue

paper plates or other stiff paper

Children will enjoy discovering natural materials and crafting them into a picture.

Preparing: Have available a variety of found materials from nature, such as twigs, leaves, and seashells, for children to examine. You will need lots of items. If possible, take children on a nature walk in a park, around the block, on a beach, or in a nearby wooded area to collect their own natural materials. For ideas on discussing and collecting natural materials, see the activity "Leaf (and Other Natural Materials) Prints" on p. 88.

Guiding the Activity: Show children a book illustrated with natural materials collages such as Eve Bunting's *Smoky Night* or Lois Ehlert's *Snowballs.* Have children choose an assortment of natural materials and arrange the items on a paper plate or stiff paper to form an interesting design or perhaps a portrait. Once they have a layout they are pleased with, they put glue on the back of each item and carefully press it to the paper. Then set the collages aside to dry, to avoid having items slip or fall off during handling.

Exploring with Children: "Did you plan your picture first and then decide which natural materials to use, or did you let the materials inspire you?" "Which materials would make a good border? Which would best represent the hair on a person's head? trees? a fence?"

Family Fun

This turkey was created using a variety of seeds, rice, candies, and macaroni.

The teacher in this primary classroom had each child take home a piece of cardboard on which she had already drawn a turkey.

Each child and his or her family created a turkey collage by filling in the turkey drawing with any natural objects they had at home. The young child who made this turkey collage had help from a very creative family!

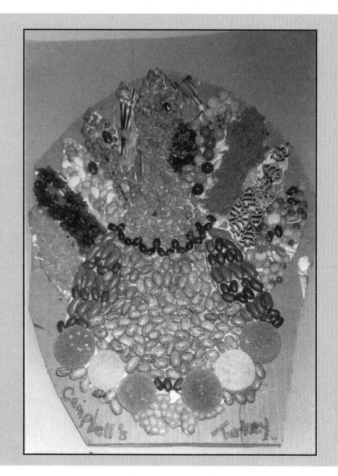

Fabric Collage

*fabric swatches in a variety of patterns, textures,
   and colors*

white glue

child-safe scissors

yarn in a variety of colors

yarn needles (plastic needles with large eyes)

*small fabric-related items, such as buttons,
   bric-a-brac, lace, ribbons, shoelaces*

construction paper (for background)

Fuzzy, bumpy, smooth, and ridged fabrics add
interest and authenticity to illustrations.

Preparing: Fabric items are something that
most families will have around the house, so
consider sending a letter home ahead of time
asking for items they would like to donate.
Other items can be purchased from or donated
by craft stores, department stores, or garage
sales.

Guiding the Activity: Show the children books
illustrated with fabric collages, such as *Tonight Is
Carnaval,* by Arthur Dorros. This story of a
Peruvian family getting ready for a carnival is
illustrated with photographs of original
arpilleras—exquisitely detailed, hand-sewn,
three-dimensional fabric pictures. Another book
illustrated beautifully with fabric collages is
Janet Bolton's *My Grandmother's Patchwork Quilt:
A Book and Pocketful of Patchwork Pieces.* This
book talks about patchwork quilting and is
illustrated entirely with patchwork fabric
collage pieces.

Have children cut pieces of fabric into
shapes for their illustrations. For example, if
they are making people, they can cut separate
hair, pants, face, and shoes; for a volcano, they
can cut a hill, smoke, and lava. Then they glue
the fabric shapes on construction paper. Children can glue on beads or other items, sew on
buttons, and stitch details with yarn. Some

children may want to outline an entire scene in yarn.

Exploring with Children: "How did you choose the
fabrics, by color or texture?" "What other items
could you add to make your collage say what you
want it to say?" "Do you plan to add some yarn
stitches to your collage?"

Variation 1: Suggest children add fabric to their
paper collages or drawings. Use of fabric textures
and prints can add visual and tactile interest. For
example, velvet can be cut in the shape of a bear or
patterned cotton can become clothing.

Variation 2: Commercial dyes can be used to dye
fabrics for collages, and the fabric can be used for
beautiful book covers.

Gadget Collage

assortment of small gadgets collected by children
white glue, tape, or staples/stapler
construction paper, cardboard, paper plates, or box lids
  (for background)

Gadgets and other "junk drawer" clutter can make interesting collages, and almost any object that is clean and in good condition is fair game. Thinking about what to use and how to arrange the objects is a creative challenge.

Preparing: Involve children in collecting an assortment of odds and ends that have interesting shapes. These might include spools, small toys, buttons, kitchen gadgets, knobs, keys, small brushes, and chains. Looking for gadgets for collages can be like a treasure hunt for children.

Guiding the Activity: Have children examine the objects, discuss their different shapes and uses, and sort and classify them by attributes such as shape, color, and texture. Classifying the objects into piles or containers provides children with a basic order for artistic possibilities. Some children may want to use a theme in their collage, such as all objects made of metal or all objects used in a kitchen. Show children a book that has illustrations made from gadgets, such as Joan Steiner's book *Look-Alikes*, in which a shoehorn becomes a slide and cobblestones are made from pennies.

Have children choose an assortment of items and arrange them on a piece of construction paper or other sturdy background material. Once they have a layout they are pleased with, they can put glue on the back of each item and affix it to the background. For objects that are difficult to affix with glue, such as a zipper, children could use tape or staples. When children are finished, set the glued collages aside to dry, to avoid having objects slip or fall off during handling.

Afterwards, give children an opportunity to share their collages and to explain what thought processes they used when they selected items.

Exploring with Children: "What are some of the different gadgets made out of?" "Can you tell what the items have been used for?" "If you were to make a collage on a theme, what are some possible themes for using the items you have available?" "If you are thinking of making a scene, what could some of your items represent?"

Variation: Primary age children will enjoy thinking like inventors with their gadgets. Ask them to examine the available items and talk with one another about how those items are typically used. Challenge children to think about how they could combine several gadgets to create a new invention.

Paper Mosaic

[paper cutter or rotary cutter]
½-inch paper squares in a variety of colors
white glue
pencils
paintbrushes
child-safe scissors
white construction paper (for background)

Mosaics are traditionally made with glass or ceramic tiles, but illustrations can be created using a mosaic approach with a variety of colors of construction paper. This technique is a version of paper collage.

Preparing: Cut different colors of construction paper into strips about ½-inch wide. Then cut across the strips at half-inch intervals to create ½-inch squares. You will need two or three sheets of colored paper, cut up, for each child.

Guiding the Activity: Discuss mosaics with children. Explain that mosaic pieces are usually small, square pieces of tile called *tesserae;* colorful glass fragments; or stones. Like a pointillist painting, a mosaic uses many small pieces of different colors to create a picture or design. (For more on this, see "Pointillism" on p. 102) Explain that the children will use the mosaic technique to create an illustration by gluing small squares of colored paper in a pattern to form their design.

Show children photographs of mosaic murals on walls and floors and explain that mosaics have been used to tell stories for thousands of years. A good book on mosaics is Elaine M. Goodwin's (1995) *Decorative Mosaics: How to Make Colorful, Imaginative Mosaics— Twelve Projects.* Some children may have seen mosaic garden stones or know someone who crafts using broken china or colored glass fragments. You can read *The Boy with Square Eyes,* by Juliet and Charles Snape, to children

and talk about how the illustrations in this book are made with mosaics.

First have children sketch their illustration in pencil on white construction paper. Then they brush glue over one small area of their illustration and, while the glue is wet, carefully affix one square at a time to fill in the image. Unlike in tissue paper collages, in mosaics the squares do not overlap. To make squares fit into small or angular areas, children will probably have to trim them to the proper shape and size with scissors.

Exploring with Children: "Are a lot of the squares the right size, or do you need to cut them before they fit where you want them to?" "Would you like to put a mosaic border around each page of writing, or would that detract from your story?"

Other Techniques

This section describes several interesting and useful techniques, including rubbings, sandpainting, and photography, that don't fall into the previous categories. It also describes how children can make their own natural dyes and paints, and even their own paper. The section concludes with a discussion of the rebus method of integrating illustrations throughout writing.

Burlap Stitchery

[sharp scissors or rotary cutter]

[wide masking tape]

yarn in a variety of colors

yarn needles (plastic needles with large eyes)

chalk (preferably as chalk pencils, but any kind works)

child-safe scissors

buttons, bric-a-brac, ribbon, lace, beads, other fabric-related materials

burlap

Working with yarn and burlap, children can use a few basic stitches to create entire illustrations.

Preparing: Burlap can be purchased by the yard at any fabric store. Cut most of the burlap into squares, one for each child, leaving some scraps for practicing. You can enclose the edges of the burlap squares in tape so the fabric doesn't unravel as children work with it.

Prepare a sampler ahead of time showing several easy stitches sewn with yarn on burlap. (Embroiderers use embroidery floss; however, children will have more success if they stitch with large yarn needles and yarn.) Some common stitches are satin stitch, backstitch, lazy daisy stitch, and French knot stitch; McAllister's *Sewing with Felt* (2003) is a good resource for children's sewing.

Guiding the Activity: Explain that stitchery has a long history as an illustration technique for creating designs, lettering, and pictures on fabrics. *Life Around the Lake,* by Maricel E. Presilla and Gloria Soto, is a perfect example of how stitchery can be used to show the everyday life of the people who create it. *Life Around the Lake,* which records the lives of the Tarascan people of Mexico, is illustrated completely with embroidered pictures created by the women of Lake Pátzcuaro. A special feature of the book is the back cover, which has photographs of the women who created the embroidered illustrations. If possible, have on hand some samples of illustrative embroidery for children to examine.

The first step is to teach children in small groups some basic stitches. Before they begin a stitchery illustration, have them practice the stitches on burlap scraps. When they are comfortable with a few stitches, they are ready to create their yarn and burlap illustrations.

Next, have children use chalk to sketch a scene on a burlap square, then use the stitches they have learned to outline and fill in their illustration. Encourage children to incorporate other sewing-related materials such as buttons, lace, and ribbons into their design.

Exploring with Children: "How do you decide which stitch to use on different parts of your illustration?" "Are there some poems and stories that go well with stitchery illustrations? What kinds of writings do not seem to work well?"

Variation 1: Challenge children to create a stitch of their own.

Variation 2: Younger children will need to stitch something large with few details, such as a rainbow or happy face. They can do this after learning just one or two of the easiest stitches such as the backstitch and satin stitch.

Crayon Texture Rubbings

crayon pieces
white typing paper

Crayon rubbings can be collected from any interesting texture. Rubbings make great backgrounds for collages.

Preparing: Broken crayons work particularly well for this activity. Peel the papers off a large selection of colored crayons.

Guiding the Activity: Before children try making their own rubbings, talk with them about the different locations and objects people find to make rubbings of. Rubbings are one way we can preserve carvings (names, other words, images) that we admire or cherish, such as inscriptions on gravestones or public monuments. Visitors take rubbings of names inscribed in the wall of the Vietnam Veterans Memorial in Washington, DC, for example. Eve Bunting's book *The Wall*, illustrated by Ronald Himler, tells about the Memorial and explores the concept of preserving memories through rubbings.

To make a crayon rubbing, children lay a sheet of paper over a surface that has an interesting texture, then rub the side of a crayon over the paper. Have children experiment with collecting rubbings from textures they find outdoors and those inside, such as a brick, fabric, rough walls, tree bark, and window screens.

Once children have collected rubbings of different textures, they can cut the rubbings into shapes to use in their illustrations. Or children can rub an entire sheet of paper to use as the background for another technique such as collage.

Exploring with Children: "Can you look at the rubbings a classmate collected and identify where they were made?" "Do some textures show up more clearly than other textures? Why do you think this happens?"

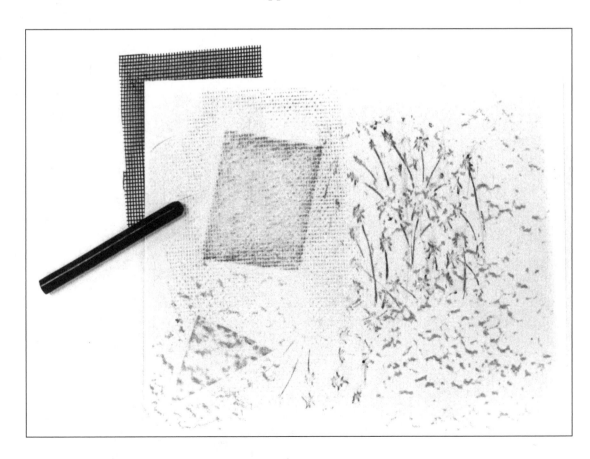

Sandpainting

sand, several colors and/or textures, in small bowls
paper cups
white glue, in a small bowl
pencils
paintbrushes
stiff paper (for background)

Sandpainting is a technique thousands of years old that traces its history to the healing ceremonies of Buddhist monks. It migrated with native North Americans from Central Asia, and remains an element of American Indian tradition among the Navajo and Hopi cultures.

Preparing: Sand for this activity can be purchased at craft stores and some discount stores in the craft department. Divide the sand into small bowls, to make it easier for children to work with.

Guiding the Activity: Explain that sand from different locations is different in texture and color. Sand from the desert or the beach may be fine, whereas sand from a hole at the side of a road may have larger, coarser grains. Navajo people, for example, make sandpaintings with the colored sands of the Southwest, sometimes adding other natural materials such as charcoal for color.

Encourage children to explore with sand. Involve them in feeling the sand by letting the grains of sand run through their fingers. Suggest they think about ways they might sift the sand into different piles and examine the grains. (A piece of screen with its edges wrapped in masking tape is one possible tool.) What differences and similarities do they find?

The first step in making a sandpainting is for children to draw their illustration on paper using a pencil. Next, they use a paintbrush dipped in glue to paint glue over the areas of their drawing that they want the sand to stick to. Then they can use a paper cup to scoop up a small portion of the sand they want to use. While the glue is still wet, they pour the sand onto the gluey surface, then set their illustration aside to dry. Once the glue has dried, they turn their illustration on end over a tray or sheet of paper,

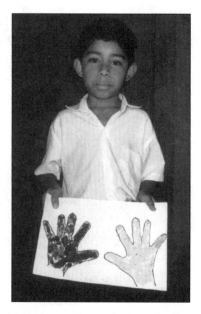

shake gently to remove the excess sand, then pour the excess back into the sand supply of that color.

For designs involving several colors, children should work with one color at a time—gluing, pouring one color, letting it dry, and collecting the excess before applying the next color.

If it's not important to keep the sand separated by color, a speedier method would have children gluing, then pouring sand carefully from a succession of cups containing various colors. Squeezing the rim of the cups almost closed will help them to achieve a very controlled pour. Children would set the completed illustration aside to dry at the very end, after pouring all the colors of excess sand into a common container.

If children want the background of their illustration to be all one color, with a picture in one or more different colors on top, the steps are slightly different. First children would apply glue over the entire paper and pour on the background sand. When this is completely dry and they have removed any excess sand, they would carefully apply glue for the new color(s) on top of the background layer by squeezing the glue *directly from the bottle* onto the background, rather than using a paintbrush. They then apply sand for the picture as explained previously.

Exploring with Children: "What type of story would a sandpainting illustrate well—a story about the beach? the desert?" "Do you know any family stories passed down from your parents or grandparents, like the Navajo stories told to Zephaniah by his father (see p. 117)?"

Traditional Navajo Sandpainting:
Telling a Story with Sand

One way to introduce the sandpainting technique is with the story of Zephaniah, told to me by Eugene Baatsoslanii Joe, who is Zephaniah's father.

Zephaniah lives with his mother and father in Shiprock, New Mexico, on the Navajo reservation. Zephaniah's grandfather was a medicine man who used traditional Navajo sandpainting in his healing ceremonies. Each sandpainting had a very special meaning and great power. The paintings were very beautiful but temporary. Because they were made for ceremonial purposes, they were destroyed shortly after they were made.

Zephaniah's father, Eugene, an artist, also paints with sand, making sandpaintings from his experiences of growing up Navajo. Eugene glues the sand onto boards so his paintings will be permanent. His work hangs in galleries and museums.

As Eugene makes his paintings, he tells Zephaniah the same Navajo stories that his father and grandfather told him when he was learning to be a sandpainter, just as his father's father did before him. Zephaniah likes to hear the stories. After Zephaniah listens to his father's stories, he makes sandpaintings of his own and tells his family his own stories that go with his paintings.

To view some of Eugene's sandpaintings and read about the art and cultural history of sandpainting, see his book with Mark Bahti, *A Guide to Navajo Sandpaintings* (2000).

Explain to children that because traditional healing designs have religious significance, many American Indians do not want the images copied for unrelated purposes. It is important for children to understand that out of respect for people's religious beliefs and practices, religious art from some cultures may be appreciated but not imitated. We can involve children in painting with sand the way the Navajo do, but children's illustrations should relate to their own experiences.

Guatemalan *Alfombras*

In many Guatemalan villages, it is a custom for a family to make an *alfombra* (Spanish for "carpet") as part of the festivities during Easter week. Like traditional Navajo sandpainting, the design and construction of these beautiful, yet so temporary, artworks have a religious significance.

Among the festival's activities is a procession in which boys, girls, men, and women carry heavy wooden carvings of Jesus and the Virgin Mary through the streets. The men dress in purple robes and the women wear their best clothing. A band at the back of the procession plays funeral music.

All of the members of a family help to create beautiful designs on the street outside their home, working quickly so they will be finished in time for the procession. These "carpets" on the streets are made from natural materials such as dyed sawdust, beans, rice, flowers, and even fruit, often laid in a bed of sand.

As the procession winds through the village, the people in the procession march right through all the beautiful carpets! It is an honor and a blessing for a family to have their carpet walked on by the procession.

Like Navajo sandpaintings, it would be disrespectful for us to duplicate the *alfombra* designs outside their religious context. But they are beautiful to learn about, and we can involve children in creating illustrations using similar techniques, such as using beans and rice in a design or gluing sawdust onto a piece of paper as the young Guatemalan boy on p. 116 did.

Photography

notebook
simple camera(s)
film

Young children enjoy taking photos. With a little help in thinking about the kinds of photographs that best tell a story, children can learn a lot about photography.

Preparing: One-time-use cameras, which are preloaded with film, can be purchased in any discount store. Or provide a point-and-shoot camera and film.

Set up a system for checking out the camera overnight, logging in each child's shots, and developing prints. The *Young Children* article "Children, Cameras, and Challenging Projects" (Savage & Holcomb 1999) offers some ideas about logistics from a similar project with second-graders.

Guiding the Activity: Explain that some illustrators who use photography on a project use black-and-white film while others use color. Share children's books containing each type of photography, and ask children to describe the different feeling each gives. Photographer Russell Freedman captures the stories of children through black-and-white photographs in his nonfiction books for young people, such as *Immigrant Kids*. One of my favorite books with color photographs of art and black-and-white photographs of children is Bruce Hucko's *Where There Is No Name for Art: The Art of Tewa Pueblo Children* (1996). Photography is an especially wonderful way to record and share history, as Don and Debra McQuiston do in *Dolls and Toys of Native America: A Journey through Childhood* (1995).

Point out how some illustrators take pictures that help tell the written story and show main events, characters, or ideas. Other books tell their story entirely in photographs, with little or no print; discuss how such photographs must be powerful and tell an entire story through just a few images.

To begin this activity, work with small groups of children, demonstrating how to load film in the camera, center an object or scene through the camera viewfinder, and snap a picture. (Don't spend time explaining how to unload the exposed film; unload the film yourself in the classroom when the last child returns the camera.) Give each child an opportunity to practice operating the camera, and show them all how you want them to record the frame number and subject of each shot. Then, before children check out the camera, remind them: Think about what you want to photograph before pointing the camera. Frame each shot carefully.

Once the film is developed and children have their prints in hand, they can talk with their classmates about the pictures and mount them in their books to illustrate their stories and poems.

Exploring with Children: "Can you hold the camera very steady while you take the picture?" "Can your friend tell from your photograph what is happening?" "What does your photograph tell the reader?"

Variation: If you have access to a digital camera, older children can use that instead. A digital camera allows a child to look at each photo immediately and decide whether to save it or shoot another.

Natural Paints

soft stones
plastic zipper bags
mallet or hammer
large rock, to scratch soft rocks on
mortar and pestle
water
liquid starch, to use as a binder
containers, to collect powder and mix paint
paintbrushes
paper

If a stone leaves a colored mark when it is scratched on a hard surface, it is of a type that can be ground into powder and made into paint. Stones can make colors such as red, brown, blue, and yellow. The most common colors would be gray, red, and various shades of brown.

Preparing: This is an outdoor activity. Adults and children should wear gloves, safety goggles, and dust masks, which can all be purchased at a hardware store.

Guiding the Activity: Take children on a field trip to collect soft stones, or have some stones available for children to examine and try. To test the suitability of any stones they find, have children scratch them on another hard surface, such as a large rock or the sidewalk. If the stones leave a colored mark, add them to the collection. Once the children have a collection of soft stones, they can sort the stones by color, putting each color into a different bag.

The next step is to smash and grind the stones into powder. Older children may be able to do this themselves under close adult supervision, but younger children should only watch an adult. To turn the soft stones into powder, you can place the stones on a hard surface, such as a concrete sidewalk, and use a mallet or hammer to smash them into small pieces and then into fine powder. Another method is to smash the stones into small pieces and then grind the pieces to powder, either with a mortar and pestle or right on the sidewalk with a hard rock.

Either way, scrape up the powder into containers, keeping the colors separated. For particularly soft stones that don't require much force, you can smash and grind the stones still sealed inside the bags—that is, strike the stones through the plastic—which makes collecting the powder very easy.

To mix the paint, children pour the powder into a container, like a jar, add water a little at a time, and stir or shake the jar until the paint is the consistency of cream. Add about one tablespoon of liquid starch per pint of paint. Children can test the paint by brushing it onto paper. If the paint rubs off too easily when it dries, it may need more liquid starch to better bind the stone particles.

Exploring with Children: "Can you think of other materials, such as clay and charcoal, you might use to make paint?" "How can you make the paint color darker?"

Variation 1: Paint can also be made with berries such as raspberries, boysenberries, or cranberries. Press about a half cup of berries through a sieve. Then add half a teaspoon of vinegar and a pinch of salt to the berry juice.

Variation 2: Tea makes tan or brown paint. Put a tea bag into about a half cup of boiling water and let it steep until the liquid is very dark brown. Remove the tea bag and discard. Let cool before using as paint.

> If some of the stones the children collect turn out not to make good paint, just encourage the children to try other stones.
>
> In science we have no failure; we just learn new things, and then we have more information to guide us the next time.

Handmade Paper

used paper
paper shredder (optional)
bucket of warm water
blender
window screen
dishpan
old, clean bedsheets, for drying paper
colander

White typing paper, newspaper, drawing paper, even glossy magazine paper can be recycled into handmade paper for wonderful child-made book covers and book pages. Used paper that has gone through a shredder works well. This is a messy activity that many young children really enjoy.

Preparing: Children can prepare for this activity by collecting used paper in a box you provide in the classroom. For a good book about papermaking, see Beth Wilkinson's *Papermaking for Kids: Simple Steps to Handcrafted Paper* (1997). Purchase a window screen at a hardware store; the screen must be small enough to fit in the dishpan, or the pan large enough to fit the screen.

Cover one or two tables in your classroom with a couple of layers of old, clean sheets for drying the fresh paper. Fill a dishpan two-thirds full of water. You will need to have a screen and blender ready near your tub.

Guiding the Activity: Talk with children about how paper is made from trees, fabric, corn-husks, rice, and even vegetables. If possible, have several different types of paper available for children to examine.

Illustrator Robert Chapman created stunning illustrations out of handmade paper for Nancy Luenn's book *A Gift for Abuelita: Celebrating the Day of the Dead.* To make the illustrations, Chapman used very thin wet paper pulp, pressing it into intricate layered molds he carved out of wood. To see another type of paper illustration, see Eve Bunting's book *Smoky Night*, illustrated by David Diaz with collages made from handmade paper.

The first step in this activity is to rip or shred the used paper, if you are not using paper that is already shredded. Have each child shred a couple of pieces of paper. They can shred more if there is not enough paper when it comes time to put it in the blender.

Next, pack an (unplugged) blender about two-thirds full with shredded paper. Add warm water until it just covers the paper. Blend the mixture until it is a fine pulp. If children want to make colored paper, they can add a two-inch square of any color of construction paper to the mixture, which will change the color of the pulp. They can even experiment with adding two or more colors to the same blender to see what color will result, such as red and blue to make purple. This blending process will need to be repeated for each child twice to yield enough pulp to make one sheet of handmade paper. The children will need varying amounts of supervision depending on their ages and maturity; an adult will always need to supervise the actual blending.

The next step is for the child to pour his or her batch of pulp into the dishpan (already two-thirds full of water; refresh as needed). Have the child swish the pulp around to suspend the pulp in the water. Then the child slides the framed screen down through the pulp suspension to the bottom of the dishpan. For this step, the child should hold the screen so that the side of the screen that is facing up in the tub is the side where the netting and the frame form a flat surface (not the side where the frame sticks up, as if the frame were the walls of a box and the netting were the floor of the box).

Next, the child lifts the screen slowly up through the suspension, keeping the screen horizontal. The netting will catch the pulp as the screen comes up through the water. Once the screen is out of the dishpan, help the child hold the screen flat and horizontal over the dishpan, so pulp caught on the netting will not slide to one edge. Have the child hold the screen flat over the tub until all the water in the suspension drains through the netting and back into the tub and quits dripping.

Now, with your help, the child turns the screen onto the sheets, so that the layer of pulp is squeezed between the sheets and the screen. With a damp kitchen sponge, the child presses into the pulp through the netting, soaking up some of the remaining water. Finally, have the child carefully pull the screen off of the pulp, leaving the fresh, new paper to dry on the sheets. Repeat all these steps with each child.

When children are finished with the activity, be sure to pour the remaining contents of the dishpan through a colander and then discard any pulp in the trash after the water has run out of it. If pulp is allowed to wash down the sink, it will clog your pipes.

While their paper dries, talk with children about the process of paper manufacturing. Help children to brainstorm all the ways we use paper every day—newspapers, magazines, mail, grocery bags, books, paper napkins, toilet paper, paper towels, tissues, sticky notes, and money. Explain that most of the paper we use daily is made from trees, and that many, many trees must be chopped down to make all those paper products. Explore with children things they can do to conserve paper so fewer trees must be processed.

Leave the pulp on the sheets until it has dried into paper, usually overnight. Once they are dry, the sheets of paper can be picked up and handled. Remind children that the paper is fragile and can be easily torn.

Exploring with Children: "When you pat the paper, can you make designs so that the paper will have more texture? What tools (for example, a fork) could you use to make a textural design? How about pushing a shoe onto the paper as it is drying, to stamp an impression of the shoe's tread?"

Variation 1: Children can add leaves, flower petals, small pieces of bark, or other small, thin natural materials to their pulp mixture before it is lifted with the screen, or they can gently push them into the surface of their paper as it dries, to add texture and visual interest to their finished paper. Alternatively, when natural materials are added to the blender and combined with the pulp, they can make interesting specks in the paper.

Variation 2: For pieces of paper with straight edges, use a mold and deckle (a special frame for paper-making) instead of a screen. Follow the steps above, holding the mold, mesh side up, with the deckle frame firmly held against the mold. After you dip the mold and deckle into the suspension, gathering the pulp, and pull it straight up from the dishpan, let the water drain. Then remove the deckle and continue the process as above.

Variation 3: Older children might like to try a process similar to the one Robert Chapman used in his illustrations for Nancy Luenn's *A Gift for Abuelita*. To make paper in molds like Chapman did, use cookie molds from the kitchen department of any discount store. To obtain the pulp, follow the same process described above, but after the pulp is blended, pour the pulp into a colander held over the sink. Once the water has dripped out, children can collect small handfuls of pulp from the colander and press them into the cookie molds. The pulp needs to be left in the mold overnight in order to dry into the shape of the mold. The next day, children can gently peel the dried paper from the inside of the mold and use the molded paper for an illustration.

Rebus Writing

markers or crayons

paper

Children substitute pictures for some words in their writings, so the illustrations are integrated into and integral to the narrative.

Preparing: On a large sheet of paper, write a story (or poem or song), but replace some of the words with pictures that you draw.

Guiding the Activity: Involve the children in reading aloud together the story you have written. Explain to them that representation of some sentences with a combination of words and pictures is a concept that originated and was popular in France in the 1700s. At that time, writing rebus notes to friends was a popular and common form of entertainment.

Challenge children to write rebus stories, poems, or songs of their own. Some children may want to try rebus writing using a verse from a song they know. Children can share their writings with their classmates, even singing together if they have illustrated a song.

Exploring with Children: "How did you decide which words to substitute pictures for?" "Are your classmates' writings easier or more difficult to read with pictures mixed in with the words? Why?"

Variation: Instead of drawing illustrations, children can combine the paper collage technique with rebus writing by cutting out pictures from magazines and gluing them into the sentences or verses.

Resources

References

Althouse, R., M.H. Johnson, & S.T. Mitchell. 2003. *The colors of learning: Integrating the visual arts into the early childhood curriculum.* New York: Teachers College Press; Washington, DC: NAEYC.

Armington, D. 1997. *The living classroom: Writing, reading, and beyond.* Washington, DC: NAEYC.

Atkinson, J.L. 1996. *Collage art: A step-by-step guide and showcase.* Gloucester, MA: Quarry Books.

Bahti, M., & E.M. Joe. 2000. *A guide to Navajo sandpainting.* Tucson, AZ: Rio Nuevo Publishers.

Bredekamp, S., & C. Copple, eds. 1997. *Developmentally appropriate practice in early childhood programs.* Rev. ed. Washington, DC: NAEYC.

Brown, M.H. 2000. Playing: The peace of childhood. *Young Children* 55 (6): 36–37.

Cadwell, L.B. 1997. *Bringing Reggio Emilia home.* New York: Teachers College Press.

Calkins, L.M. 1994. *The art of teaching and writing.* Portsmouth, NH: Heinemann.

Capezzuto, S.M., & D.A. DaRos-Voseles. 2001. Using experts to enhance classroom projects. *Young Children* 56 (2): 84–85.

Cocking, R.R., & C. Copple. 1987. Social influences on representational awareness, plans for representing, and plans as representation. In *Blueprints for thinking: The role of planning in cognitive development,* eds. S.L. Friedman, E.K. Scholnick, & R.R. Cocking, 428–65. Cambridge, England: Cambridge University Press.

Dudley-Marling, C., & D. Searle. 1991. *When students have time to talk: Creating contexts for learning language.* Portsmouth, NH: Heinemann.

Dyson, A.H. 1993. *Social worlds of children learning to write in an urban primary school.* New York: Teachers College Press.

Edwards, C., L. Gandini, & G. Forman, eds. 1998. *The hundred languages of children: The Reggio Emilia approach—Advanced reflections.* Greenwich, CT: Ablex.

Engel, B.S. 1995. *Considering children's art: Why and how to value their works.* Washington, DC: NAEYC.

Forman, G., & B. Fyfe. 1998. Negotiated learning through design, documentation, and discourse. In *The hundred languages of children: The Reggio Emilia approach—Advanced reflections*, eds. C. Edwards, L. Gandini, & G. Forman, 239–60. Greenwich, CT: Ablex.

Goodwin, E.M. 1995. *Decorative mosaics: How to make colorful, imaginative mosaics—Twelve projects*. New York: Owl Books.

Graves, D.H. 1983. *Writing: Teachers and children at work*. Portsmouth, NH: Heinemann.

Harste, J., & K.G. Short. 1991. Literature circles and literature response activities. In *Literacy in progress*, eds. B.M. Power & R. Hubbard, 191–202. Portsmouth, NH: Heinemann.

Head Start Bureau. 2003. *The Head Start leaders' guide to positive child outcomes: Strategies to support positive child outcomes*, 114–18. Washington, DC: U.S. Department of Health and Human Services, Administration for Children and Families.

Helm, J., S. Beneke, & K. Steinheimer. 1998. *Windows on learning: Documenting young children's work*. New York: Teachers College Press.

Hendrick, J., ed. 1997. *First steps toward teaching the Reggio way*. Upper Saddle River, NJ: Prentice-Hall.

Hilliker, J. 1998. Labeling to beginning narrative. In *Understanding writing: Ways of observing, learning, and teaching*, 2d ed., eds. T. Newkirk & N. Atwell, 14–22. Portsmouth, NH: Heinemann.

Hucko, B. 1996. *Where there is no name for art: The art of Tewa Pueblo children*. Santa Fe, NM: School of American Research Press.

Hughes, F.P. 1999. *Children, play, and development*. Needham Heights, MA: Allyn & Bacon.

Isenberg, J.P., & M.R. Jalongo. 1997. *Creative expression and play in early childhood*. 2d ed. Columbus, OH: Merrill.

Jalongo, M.R. 2003. *Early childhood language arts*. Boston: Allyn & Bacon.

Jalongo, M.R. 2004. *Young children and picture books*. 2d ed. Washington, DC: NAEYC.

Jones, E., & G. Reynolds. 1992. *The play's the thing. . . . Teachers' roles in children's play*. New York: Teachers College Press.

Katz, L. 1990. Impressions of Reggio Emilia preschools. *Young Children* 45 (2): 11–12.

Katz, L., & S. Chard. 1996. *Engaging children's minds: The project approach*. Norwood, NJ: Ablex.

Kieff, J.E., & R.M. Casbergue. 2000. *Playful learning and teaching: Integrating play into preschool and primary programs*. Boston: Allyn & Bacon.

Krashen, S. 1997. *Every person a reader: An alternative to the California Task Force Report on Reading*. Portsmouth, NH: Heinemann.

Matthews, K. 2002. Building a community of experience. *Young Children* 57 (6): 86–89.

McAllister, B. 2003. *Sewing with felt: Learn basic stitches to create more than 60 colorful projects*. Photographs by H. Schneider. Honesdale, PA: Boyds Mills Press.

McQuiston, D., & D. McQuiston. 1995. *Dolls and toys of native America: A journey through childhood.* San Francisco, CA: Chronicle Books.

Neuman, S.B., C. Copple, & S. Bredekamp. 2000. *Learning to read and write: Developmentally appropriate practice for young children.* Washington, DC: NAEYC.

Paley, V. 1981. *Wally's stories.* Cambridge, MA: Harvard University Press.

Paley, V. 1990. *The boy who would be a helicopter: The uses of storytelling in the classroom.* Cambridge, MA: Harvard University Press.

Piaget, J. 1951. *Play, dreams, and imitation in childhood.* New York: Norton.

Savage, M., & D. Holcomb. 1999. Children, cameras, and challenging projects. *Young Children* 54 (2): 27–29.

Schickedanz, J. 1999. *Much more than the ABCs: The early stages of reading and writing.* Washington, DC: NAEYC.

Schirrmacher, R. 2002. *Art and creative development for young children.* 4th ed. Albany, NY: Delmar.

Sutton-Smith, B. 1967. The role of play in cognitive development. *Young Children* 22: 361–70.

Taunton, M., & C. Colbert. 2000. Art in the early childhood classroom: Authentic experiences and extended dialogues. In *Promoting meaningful learning: Innovations in educating early childhood professionals,* ed. N.J. Yelland, 67–76. Washington, DC: NAEYC.

Thompson, S.C. 2001. *Celebrating the world of work: Interviews and activities.* Portsmouth, NH: Teacher Ideas Press.

Vygotsky, L. 1978. *Mind in society: Development of higher psychological processes.* Cambridge, MA: Harvard University Press.

Wilkinson, B. 1997. *Papermaking for kids: Simple steps to handcrafted paper.* Salt Lake City, UT: Gibbs Smith.

Wright, S. 1997. Learning how to learn: The arts as core in an emergent curriculum. *Childhood Education* 73 (6): 361–66.

Children's Literature Cited

17 Kings and 42 Elephants. Margaret Mahy; illustrated by Patricia MacCarthy.

Abuela. Arthur Dorros; illustrated by Elisa Kleven.

The Amazing Potato: A Story in Which the Incas, Conquistadors, Marie Antoinette, Thomas Jefferson, Wars, Famines, Immigrants, and French Fries All Play a Part. Milton Meltzer.

Anno's Journey. Mitsumasa Anno.

Anno's Magic Seeds. Mitsumasa Anno.

Anno's USA. Mitsumasa Anno.

The Boy with Square Eyes. Juliet Snape and Charles Snape.

Brown Bear, Brown Bear, What Do You See? Bill Martin, Jr.; illustrated by Eric Carle.

The Cowboy and the Black-Eyed Pea. Tony Johnston; illustrated by Warren Ludwig.

Dinosaurumpus! Tony Mitton; illustrated by Guy Parker-Rees.

The Doorbell Rang. Pat Hutchins.

Elizabeti's Doll. Stephanie Stuve-Bodeen; illustrated by Christy Hale.

Faith Ringgold: Portraits of Women Artists for Children. Robyn Montana Turner.

Gabriela's Beautiful Carpet / La Bella Alfrombra de Gabriela. Keith Thompson and Susan Thompson; illustrated by Rosalie Thompson (Guatemala City, Vista Publications).

General Store. Rachel Field; illustrated by Giles Laroche.

The Gettysburg Cyclorama: Portrayal of the High Tide of the Confederacy. Dean S. Thomas.

A Gift for Abuelita: Celebrating the Day of the Dead. Nancy Luenn; illustrated by Robert Chapman.

The Giving Tree. Shel Silverstein.

The Goat in the Rug as Told to Charles L. Blood & Martin Link by Geraldine. Charles L. Blood and Martin A. Link; illustrated by Nancy Winslow Parker.

The Hat. Jan Brett.

Hattie and the Fox. Mem Fox; illustrated by Patricia Mullins.

If a Bus Could Talk: The Story of Rosa Parks. Faith Ringgold.

Immigrant Kids. Russell Freedman.

In the Hollow of Your Hand: Slave Lullabies. Alice McGill; illustrated by Michael Cummings.

Joseph Had a Little Overcoat. Simms Taback.

Keep the Lights Burning, Abbie. Peter Roop and Connie Roop; illustrated by Peter E. Hanson.

The Legend of the Bluebonnet: An Old Tale of Texas Retold and Illustrated by Tomie De Paola. Tomie De Paola.

Life around the Lake. Maricel E. Presilla and Gloria Soto.

Little Cloud. Eric Carle.

Little Herder in Autumn. Ann Nolan Clark; illustrated by Hoke Denetsosie.

The Little Old Lady Who Was Not Afraid of Anything. Linda Williams; illustrated by Megan Lloyd.

The Little Red Hen (Makes a Pizza). Philemon Sturges; illustrated by Amy Walrod.

Little Red Riding Hood. Candice Ransom; illustrated by Tammie Lyon.

Lon Po Po: A Red-Riding Hood Story from China. Ed Young.

Look-Alikes. Joan Steiner; photography by Thomas Lindley.

Look What I Did with a Leaf. Morteza E. Sohi.

Lunchtime for a Purple Snake. Harriet Ziefert; illustrated by Todd McKie.

Mama Provi and the Pot of Rice. Sylvia Rosa-Casanova; illustrated by Robert Roth.

The Man Who Planted Trees. Jean Giono; illustrated by Michael McCurdy.

Mary Wore Her Red Dress and Henry Wore His Green Sneakers. Merle Peek.

Monster Mama. Liz Rosenberg; illustrated by Stephen Gammell.

More Potatoes! Millicent E. Selsam; illustrated by Ben Shecter.

The Mud Pony. Caron Lee Cohen; illustrated by Shonto Begay.

My Grandmother's Patchwork Quilt: A Book and Pocketful of Patchwork Pieces. Janet Bolton.

My Name Is Georgia. Jeanette Winter.

My Prairie Year: Based on the Diary of Elenore Plaisted. Brett Harvey; illustrated by Deborah Kogan Ray.

Nursery Tales around the World. Judy Sierra; illustrated by Stefano Vitale.

One Potato: A Counting Book of Potato Prints. Diana Pomeroy.

Pancakes, Pancakes! Eric Carle.

The Polar Express. Chris Van Allsburg.

The Rainbow Fish. Marcus Pfister.

Red Leaf, Yellow Leaf. Lois Ehlert.

Rooster's Off to See the World. Eric Carle.

Shadow. Marcia Brown.

Sing a Song of People. Lois Lenski; illustrated by Giles Laroche.

Smoky Night. Eve Bunting; illustrated by David Diaz.

Snowballs. Lois Ehlert.

The Snowman. Raymond Briggs.

The Snowy Day. Ezra Jack Keats.

Stories to Solve: Folktales from around the World. George Shannon; illustrated by Caldecott Honer and Peter Sis.

Swimmy. Leo Lionni.

The Tiny Seed. Eric Carle.

There Was an Old Lady Who Swallowed a Fly. Simms Taback.

This Old Man. Carol Jones.

Tonight Is Carnaval. Arthur Dorros.

Tortillas para Mamá and Other Nursery Rhymes. Margot C. Griego; illustrated by Barbara Cooney.

The Very Hungry Caterpillar. Eric Carle.

The Wall. Eve Bunting; illustrated by Ronald Himler.

Whistle for Willie. Ezra Jack Keats.

Window. Jeannie Baker.

Wood. Christin Ditchfield.

Websites and Organizations

The Children's Book Council, Author/Illustrator Directory
www.cbcbooks.org/contacts. Links to selected children's book authors and illustrators.

The Children's Literature Web Guide
www.acs.ucalgary.ca/~dkbrown. Internet resources related to books for children and young adults, including links to the Doucette Library of Teaching Resources, updates of new releases in children's literature, and discussion groups.

Children's Picture Book Database at Miami University
www.lib.muohio.edu/pictbks. Abstracts of more than 5,000 children's picture books, with extensive search capabilities.

Index to Internet Sites: Children's and Young Adults' Authors and Illustrators
http://falcon.jmu.edu/~ramseyil/biochildhome.htm. Links to author and illustrator sites, as well as links to other sites with information on author/illustrator appearances and interviews, teacher resource information, name pronunciation, and more.

International Reading Association
www.reading.org. Professional membership organization of those involved in teaching reading to learners of all ages.

National Art Education Association
www.naea-reston.org. Professional membership organization for art educators of all levels and others in the field.

National Association for the Education of Young Children
www.naeyc.org. The world's largest early childhood education organization, with a national network of local, state, and regional Affiliates dedicated to bringing high-quality early learning opportunities to all children from birth through age eight.

Reading Is Fundamental
www.rif.org. An extensive children's and family nonprofit literacy organization that delivers free books and literacy resources to children and families in need.

Society of Children's Book Writers and Illustrators
www.scbwi.org. Community of people who write, illustrate, or share a vital interest in children's literature; website includes discussion boards, links to publishing resources, and other member services.

VSA Arts (formerly Very Special Arts)
www.vsarts.org. Nonprofit organization offering publications, guides, and other resources on a wide variety of subject matter in arts and education relating to students, artists, and audiences with disabilities.

For Further Reading

Brown, M.H. 2000. Playing: The peace of childhood. *Young Children* 55 (6): 36–37.

Edwards, B. 1999. *Drawing on the right side of the brain: A course in enhancing creativity and artistic confidence.* New York: Putnam.

Engel, B.S. 1995. *Considering children's art: Why and how to value their works.* Washington, DC: NAEYC.

Epstein, A.S., & E. Trimis. 2002. *Supporting young artists: The development of the visual arts in young children.* Ypsilanti, MI: High/Scope.

Garvey, C. 1990. *Play.* Cambridge, MA: Harvard University Press.

Greenberg, P. 1999. Listening to children talk while they draw. *Young Children* 54 (6): 13.

Greenberg, P. 1999. Painting every day. *Young Children* 54 (5): 81.

Hirsch, E.D., Jr. 1998. *Cultural literacy: What every American needs to know.* New York: Vintage Books.

Jones, J., & R. Courtney. 2004. Documenting early science learning. *Young Children* 57 (5): 34–40.

Koster, J.B. 1999. Clay for little fingers. *Young Children* 54 (2): 18–22.

Lasky, L., & R. Mukerii-Bergeson. 1990. *Art: Basic for young children.* Washington, DC: NAEYC.

McAfee, O., D.J. Leong, & E. Bodrova. 2004. *Basics of assessment: A primer for early childhood educators.* Washington, DC: NAEYC.

Power, B.M., & R. Hubbard. 1991. *Literacy in process: The Heinemann reader.* Portsmouth, NH: Heinemann.

Reynolds, G., & E. Jones. 1997. *Master players: Learning from children at play.* New York: Teachers College Press.

Rogers, C.S., & J.K. Sawyers. 1988. *Play in the lives of children.* Washington, DC: NAEYC.

Zimmerman, E., & L. Zimmerman. 2000. Research in review. Art education and early childhood education: The young child as creator and meaning maker within a community context. *Young Children* 55 (6): 87–92.

Developmental Benchmarks and Stages for Ages 4-8: Appropriate Arts Activities

Stages	Ages	Examples of What Children Do During This Stage
PRESCHOOLERS		
Preschoolers learn greatly from interaction with others. They begin to understand that they have feelings and opinions that are different from those of others. Children at this stage are more likely to understand and remember the relationships, concepts, and strategies that they acquire through firsthand, meaningful experience. They have longer attention spans and enjoy activities that involve exploring, investigating, and stretching their imagination.	4 to 5 years	• Can copy simple geometric figures, dress self, and use more sophisticated utensils. • Use language to express thinking and increasingly complex sentences in speaking to others. Express their own feelings when listening to stories. • Enjoy using words in rhymes and understand nonsense and using humor. • Can be very imaginative and like to exaggerate. • Say and begin writing the alphabet. • Can identify what is missing from a picture (such as a face without a nose). • Can identify basic colors. • Have better control in running, jumping, and hopping but tend to be clumsy.
SCHOOL-AGE CHILDREN		
School-age children are able to make conscious decisions about art, music, dance, and theater and respond to them with feelings and emotion. They learn to compare and contrast different sounds, pictures, and movements. They become increasingly skilled at creating their own art, songs, stories, and dance movements. Since children learn in an integrated fashion, it is vital that their learning experiences incorporate multiple domains of development including cognitive, physical, and socioemotional.	5 to 8 years	• Have good body control for doing cartwheels and better balance for learning to ride a bike. • Play jump rope and hopscotch. • Can build inventive model buildings from cardboard and other materials. • Begin spelling and writing, and enjoy telling stories to other children and adults. • Become increasingly independent and try new activities on their own.

Children as Illustrators

Sample Arts Experiences That Promote Learning	What Adults and Children Can Do Together
Continue previous experiences (for younger children), as well as the following:	*Continue previous experiences (for younger children), as well as the following:*
• Strengthen nonverbal, cognitive skills by encouraging children to describe people in their world using pictures, body movements, and mime. • Provide creative outlets for prereading skills through activities such as making up stories, reciting poems, and singing songs with puppets and stuffed animals. • Children begin to make observations by role-playing human and animal characters in a variety of imaginary settings. • Memory is strengthened by repeating stories, poems, and songs. • By using clay or other art supplies, children learn to make choices and how to make things happen.	• Discover with children how the body can move to music and the difference when there is no music. • Create music with children using empty containers as drums. (Empty plastic containers filled with dried beans and rice can serve as maracas, for example.) • Make a patchwork quilt with scraps of materials sewn together with yarn. Create and illustrate stories based on the quilt. • Encourage children to assume roles of family members or literary figures in improvisations. Base them on children's experiences, family customs, books, or songs. • Re-create drawings from favorite books.
• Children will learn many ways of using their own language to tell stories. This can be encouraged by telling folktales and stories through pantomime, drawing, and music. • Through the artistic process, children learn what works and what doesn't. They also learn how to think about making choices when experiencing music, dance, theater, and art. • Children develop higher levels of thinking by learning to look at others' artwork or performances and developing an opinion. • When discussing music, art, dance, and theater, children can talk in terms of likes and dislikes. This builds judgment and analytical skills.	• Represent familiar actions like making pizza and doing chores in creative movement and dance activities. Allow the children to choose movements and ask the reasons for their choices. • Write and recite poetry and paint pictures that depict themes such as nature, school, and family. Ask questions and encourage discussion. • Exhibit children's artwork, and hang it so others can look at and respond to it. • Make scrapbooks or portfolios to keep favorite stories, photos, and artwork. • Collect tapes and recordings of music and encourage children to select favorites. • Encourage improvisation and stories, and provide materials that offer imaginary props.

Source: Excerpted and adapted from *Young Children and the Arts: Making Creative Connections*, a report of the Task Force on Children's Learning and the Arts: Birth to Age Eight and Sara Goldhawk. A product of the Arts Education Partnership, pp. 6-13. Visit http://aep-arts.org.

Early years are learning years

Become a member of NAEYC, and help make them count!

Just as you help young children learn and grow, the National Association for the Education of Young Children—your professional organization—supports you in the work you love. NAEYC is the world's largest early childhood education organization, with a national network of local, state, and regional Affiliates. We are more than 100,000 members working together to bring high-quality early learning opportunities to all children from birth through age eight.

Since 1926, NAEYC has provided educational services and resources for people working with children, including:

• *Young Children*, the award-winning journal (six issues a year) for early childhood educators

• **Books, posters, brochures, and videos** to support your work with young children and families

• **The NAEYC Annual Conference**, which brings tens of thousands of people together from across the country and around the world to share their expertise and ideas on the education of young children

• **Insurance plans** for members and programs

• **A voluntary accreditation system** to help programs reach national standards for high-quality early childhood education

• **Young Children International** to promote global communication and information exchanges

• **www.naeyc.org**—a dynamic Website with up-to-date information on all of our services and resources

To join NAEYC

To find a complete list of membership benefits and options or to join NAEYC online, visit **www.naeyc.org/membership.** Or you can mail this form to us.

(Membership must be for an individual, not a center or school.)

Name_____

Address_____

City_____ State_____ ZIP_____

E-mail _____

Phone (H) _____ (W)_____

❒ New member

❒ Renewal ID #_____

Affiliate name/number _____

To determine your dues, you must visit **www.naeyc.org/membership** or call 800-424-2460, ext. 2002.

Indicate your payment option

❒ VISA   ❒ MasterCard

Card # _____

Exp. date_____

Cardholder's name _____

Signature _____

Note: By joining NAEYC you also become a member of your state and local Affiliates.

Send this form and payment to

NAEYC
PO Box 97156
Washington, DC 20090-7156